THE FORTH AT WAR

William F. Hendrie

THE FORTH AT WAR

Birlinn

To my uncles Andrew Strachan and Douglas Snedden, who both gave the years of their youth to fight for their country in the army and the RAF respectively during the Second World War. The sacrifice which they, and so many like them, made must never be forgotton.

First published in 2002 by
Birlinn Limited
West Newington House
10 Newington Road
Edinburgh
EH9 1QS

www.birlinn.co.uk

ISBN 1 84158 183 6

British Library Cataloguing-in-Publication Data
A catalogue record for this book is available from the British Library

Series design: James Hutcheson
Layout and origination: Mark Blackadder

Printed and bound in Great Britain by the Bath Press, Glasgow

CONTENTS

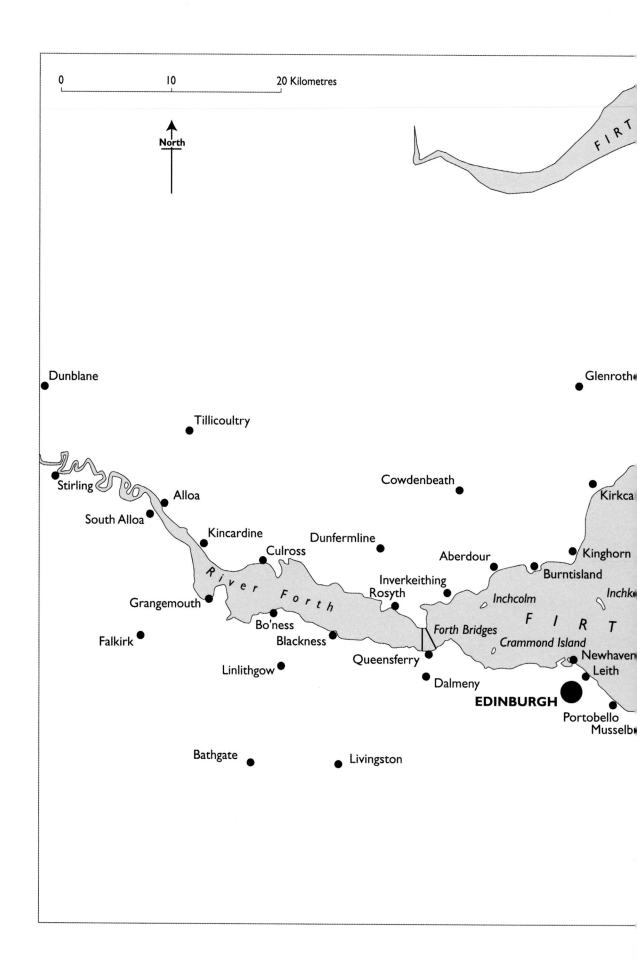

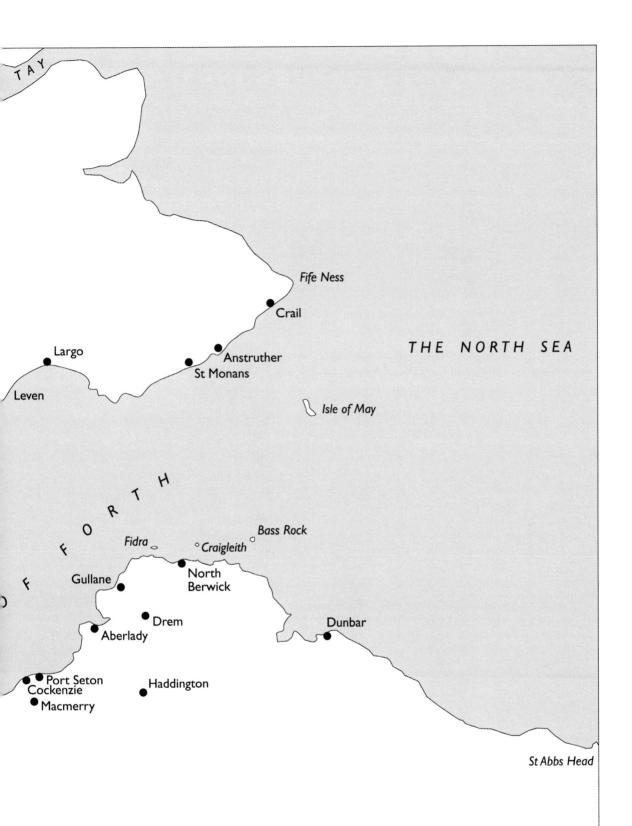

ILLUSTRATION CREDITS

All illustrations are reproduced by permission of The Imperial War Museum, except in the following cases, where permission has been granted by:

Sandy Burnett (Fig. 146)

Bill Cochrane (Fig. 63)

John Doherty (Fig. 146)

William F. Hendrie (Fig. 3)

Dunfermline Library (Figs 48, 49, 150)

The Royal Commission on the Ancient and Historical Monuments of Scotland (Figs. 23, 24, 25, 28, 29, 59, 64, 84, 141, 149, 151)

All pictures from the Imperial War Museum and The Royal Commission on the Ancient and Historical Monuments of Scotland are Crown copyright.

INTRODUCTION

Since the days when heavily-laden galleys docked at Cramond, bringing vitally needed provisions and equipment to supply the Roman army manning the Antonine Wall, the River Forth and its estuary or firth, as it is usually known, have together played a vital role in every conflict affecting the country down through the centuries.

The word firth, derived from the same root as the Norwegian 'fjord', is itself a link with the Vikings, who in the Middle Ages regularly raided the settlements along the shores of the Forth until their defeat by Macbeth at the Battle of Kinghorn. After the battle, the Norsemen paid Danegeld to be allowed to bury their warriors on the island of Inchcolm, which, even at this early date, was clearly recognised as a holy place. The strangely hog-backed tombstone on the grassy hillside towards the west end of this islet is believed to mark the grave of one of the Viking warlords.

Inchcolm takes its name from the Gaelic word for island and St Colm, to whom it is dedicated. After the Black Fathers of the Augustine Order built the impressive twelfth-century abbey for which it is now famous, it was attacked on several further occasions, this time by the English, who were attracted by the rich horde of gold and silver communion vessels which the church was known to possess. The most ferocious of these raids occurred in 1384. The abbey was set alight and a contemporary account states that it was only saved by a miraculously fortuitous change in the direction of the wind, which blew the flames back on the raiders, who were driven off by the suffocating smoke. The final English attack on Inchcolm did not take place until 1547, when, following the Scottish defeat at the Battle of Pinkie during what was known as the Rough Wooing of Mary, Queen of Scots, it was garrisoned for a time by troops under the command of the Earl of Somerset.

From the late 1400s, however, the English who ventured into the firth had to reckon with the prowess of Scotland's most famous fifteenth-century skipper, Sir Andrew Wood of Largo, who, in the days before the creation of a Scottish navy, used his own merchant ships, the *Flower* and the *Yellow Caravel*, to keep the Auld Enemy in check. Sir Andrew, whose exploits have

Fig. 2

Rosyth Castle guarded the shoreline of the River Forth at this spot on the Fife coast for centuries before the building of the Royal Naval Dockyard. It is now under the care of Historic Scotland and perhaps now that Rosyth is no longer a naval base, public access may be permitted at some future date.

The ruin on the left is that of a pigeon loft, or doocot, as it was known, which kept the castle's residents supplied with fresh meat during the winter when other sources were scarce. The three-storey castle building seen here was erected in 1561 and replaced an earlier building.

been recorded in Lindsay of Pitscottie's *Historie and Chronicles of Scotland*, was always ready to lend his vessels to support his monarch, James III. In 1488 he played a leading role in ferrying both troops and supplies up the Forth prior to the Battle of Sauchie. Despite his efforts, however, the fight was lost and King James was treacherously murdered.

James III's son and successor, James IV, determined to deter the English by making Sir Andrew the commander of a Scottish navy and by providing him with the greatest battleship ever built. The stranding of Sir Andrew's *Yellow Caravel* on a sandbank, which barred the entrance to the existing port of Leith, decided the king that his new warship must face no such risk. He therefore ordered the construction of an entire new shipbuilding yard slightly further upriver, at what had until then been a quiet little fishing harbour known as St Mary's Port because of its chapel dedicated to the Virgin Mary. In 1504 work began on the excavation of a graving dock; the earth and rubble from it was used to form a protective breakwater and the foundations for a pier at what became known as the New Haven. At the same time, 163 trees from along the banks of the tributary of the Forth, the Water of Leith, were felled and brought to the site to build homes for the hundreds of joiners and other craftsmen who were required first to construct this new naval dockyard and then the ship which it was designed to build. By 1507 the workshops, warehouses and a very vital rope works were complete and all was ready for the laying of the keel of what was to become the *Great Michael*.

Sir David Lindsay, the author of *Ane Satyre of the Thrie Estaitis*, described how every oak in the woods in Fife, except those surrounding Falkland Palace, which formed the royal hunting grounds, was felled in order to find a tree-trunk long and strong and straight enough for the keel. More timber was imported from the forests of Scandinavia, while canvas for the sails was fetched from France and the whole of Europe was scoured for all of the items of chandlery required to fit out such a large vessel – from anchors to lanterns and from compasses to guns. For the next four years, New Haven Port of Grace, as it was by then known, became the largest employer of labour Scotland had ever known. As the *Great Michael* neared completion her four tall masts became a local landmark. Then, finally, at Michaelmas 1511, in the presence of King James and his young English queen, Margaret, the *Great Michael* took to the water for the first time. Following the launch, the king and the royal party were rowed out to the ship as she rode at anchor. In the evening all those who had helped to build her were invited on board and entertained at a celebration party, which continued on her lantern-lit decks until well into the night.

One of the reasons James chose Newhaven for the building of the *Great Michael* was that he wanted personally to supervise her fitting-out, and he is said to have taken great pride over the next six months in visiting her every day as the work progressed. By March 1512 she was sufficiently far advanced to be towed out into the firth by the local fishermen, who then went on to tow her all the way up the Forth to the other Scottish royal naval dockyard at Airth. That site is now a green field; much land has been reclaimed from the river and it is hard to imagine so large and impressive a sailing ship there. But there it was that painters and other finishing tradesmen laboured on her for a further year. At last, in March 1513, she voyaged back down the Forth under her own sails to Newhaven, where she was dry-docked. This was done by sailing her into the dock where she had been built, then damming the entrance behind her tall stern and painstakingly baling out all the water. After this overhaul, she finally sailed out into the firth and took up station for the first time in the lee of the largest of the Forth islands, Inchkeith, ready to deter any English invader who dared enter her territory. Although James had wed Margaret at the 'Marriage of the Thistle and the Rose' in an attempt to bring peace to their two lands, he had already been persuaded to go to war with his English in-laws to support Scotland's Auld Alliance with the French. Soon he and most of his young Scottish nobles lay slain at the Battle of Flodden in unlucky 1513.

The ill-fated monarch was succeeded by his son, who became James V, and it was during his reign that the Forth's most famous shore-side fortification, Blackness Castle, situated on the south side of the river between Bo'ness and Queensferry, acquired its nickname of Scotland's 'ship-shaped' castle. It was said that James' Admiral of the Fleet, Archibald Douglas, designed it as a stone-walled man o' war, complete with a solid stern tower, a main-mast tower and a wave-lapped bow tower, so that he could have a land-based flagship rather than face the discomfort of the seasickness from which he suffered every time he was forced actually to set sail. Blackness was itself the subject of several naval bombardments when, during the reign of James V's daughter, Mary, Queen of Scots, it was garrisoned by her French supporters and therefore attacked by her English enemies. During the same troubled period, following the defeat of the Scots at the Battle of Pinkie in 1547, the island of Inchkeith was seized by a detachment of English soldiers under the Earl of Somerset. They held it for two years until, in 1549, they were dislodged by a combined force of Scottish and French troops. The island was garrisoned by Mary's French allies until her return to Scotland in 1560. In 1564, Mary, her ladies-in-waiting and her French courtiers paid a royal visit to Inchkeith, an occasion still marked by a commemorative plaque

Fig. 3

Blackness Castle on the Lothian shore of the River Forth between Bo'ness and Queensferry is often nicknamed Scotland's 'ship-shaped' castle.

situated near the island's hilltop lighthouse. When Mary later abdicated in favour of her infant son, King James VI, the fact that the island had provided the French with such a stronghold in the Forth prompted the first parliament of his reign to order that all the fortifications on Inchkeith should be demolished so that it could never again be used in this manner.

However, Inchkeith was again fortified 200 years later during the panic which swept Scotland when the population feared invasion by Napoleonic forces. Gun emplacements were established on three of the island's headlands; they were linked by a one-and-a-half-mile-long military road defended by deep dry moats twenty feet wide and twenty feet deep. Four nineteen-pound guns were installed on the island, two on the southern battery and one each on the northern and north-western emplacements. The guns were designed deliberately to fire over the four-foot-high parapet walls, not through loopholes in them, so that they could turn through 360 degrees to fire in any direction from which an attack was mounted.

During this period, Leith, on the shore opposite Inchkeith, also enjoyed the protection of a Martello-style tower similar to those hurriedly erected around the south and east coast of England because of fear of invasion by Napoleon. But Leith's shore-side fort resulted from the earlier threat posed by the Scottish-born turncoat privateer John Paul Jones, who in 1779 sailed into the Firth of Forth in support of the colonists during the American War of Independence. Fortunately for the inhabitants of Edinburgh's port, a fierce westerly gale swept the privateer out into the North Sea and he did not return to try to mount a second attack. But the threat which he had posed was sufficient for the inhabitants to demand better protection. This resulted in a contract for James Craig, the young architect whose design won the competition for the layout of the New Town of Edinburgh, but who had had little work ever since because of his conceited pomposity. Instead of designing the broad streets, curving crescents and circuses of the Georgian city, he was now called upon to draw up plans for Leith Fort, of which only a small section of the thick walls and two guardhouses now survive.

Some earlier Leith defences can also be seen on Leith Links, the green sward which is a pleasant feature of the east end of the port. These earthworks were hurriedly thrown up in 1560 when Leith, the last bastion of Catholicism in Scotland, was besieged by both the Scottish and English armies. One of the fortifications is known as the Giant's Brae and was raised as a gun battery by the English troops so that they could fire over the town wall at the buildings in Constitution Street. The other earthwork is called Lady Fyfe's Brae and was the site of Pelham's Battery. Although the siege of Leith ended peacefully after the death of Mary, Queen of Scots' mother, Mary of Guise, in the meantime most of the old buildings in Leith had been destroyed by the bombardment from these two defensive positions.

Leith again saw action a century later, when, following the execution of King Charles I in 1649, the troops of General Leslie built Leith Walk as a military road to link the port with the centre of Edinburgh. When Oliver Cromwell subsequently invaded Scotland during the period of the Republic, he again garrisoned the town and fortified it under General Monk. At the end of the street, opposite Leith's former customs house, can still be seen the remains of the fortress constructed at that time.

[1]

THE FIRST WORLD WAR

ROSYTH ROYAL NAVAL DOCKYARD

It was fitting that the Firth of Forth was the scene for a dramatic event at the end of the First World War. Ten days after the Armistice of 11 November 1918, the vessels of the German fleet finally sailed in to surrender. The Forth had played a major role throughout the latter stages of the hostilities, yet at the outset of the war this had not been anticipated by the Lords of the Admiralty. Indeed, since the nineteenth century, the attitude of the naval chiefs in distant Whitehall had been ambivalent as to the use of the Forth as a major anchorage for the British fleet.

At the time of the Napoleonic Wars, Admiral Lord Keith of Tulliallan (near Kincardine Bridge) tried to persuade his superiors at the Admiralty that Scotland should have a naval base and that his Fife estate would make an ideal setting, with a dockyard at Longannet (where the tall chimney of the coal-fired electricity power station now dominates the skyline). But their lordships decided that their wooden-hulled men o' war could be adequately victualled while lying off-shore at Queensferry and Lord Keith's proposals were taken no further, despite receiving support from another Scottish admiral, George Hope of Carriden House. The house was situated overlooking the river between Bo'ness and Blackness. Hope commanded HMS *Defence* at the Battle of Trafalgar in 1805 and was later appointed chief of the British navy in the Baltic.

Admiral Hope's son James followed in his father's wake and also went to sea. When he in turn became an admiral, he too campaigned to give the Royal Navy a more Scottish identity in order to improve recruitment. His suggestions included naming ships of the line after Scottish places so that potential recruits would identify with them in the same way that they already did with famous Scottish military regiments. He also designed a new Scottish naval uniform complete with a tartan-trimmed Balmoral bonnet, which the men on his own flagship actually wore for a time during the China Campaign. It was during this voyage to the Far East that the enterprising

Scottish admiral also introduced the idea of amateur theatricals to keep his
crew occupied during long days at sea. These dramas were performed on the
main deck and the admiral's favourite was a staging of Sir Walter Scott's *Rob
Roy*, which provided plenty of action and stirring fights for the sailors who
played the parts. It proved so successful that Admiral Hope presented it on
several future occasions when his ship was in port, for the entertainment of
expatriate British merchants and their families, who were invited aboard for
the occasion.

Interest in a stronger Scottish connection with the Royal Navy was
revived half a century later when, during the 1880s, the opening of the Kiel
Canal created a great deal of interest in Britain. The success of the canal in
linking the Baltic port of Kiel with the River Elbe, providing the Kaiser's navy
with a short cut to the German Ocean (as the North Sea was then proudly
known), led to speculation about the possibility of constructing a similarly
massive waterway across the narrow waist of central Scotland to replace the
existing eighteenth-century Forth and Clyde Canal. This would permit equal
manoeuvrability between the Atlantic and the North Sea for the British Navy.

The successful campaign for the building of the Manchester Ship Canal
further fuelled the campaign for a Scottish Ship Canal or Naval Canal, as it
was sometimes described. In connection with the idea of naval use, it was
even suggested that, instead of keeping to the 39-mile route of the existing
canal between Grangemouth on the Forth and Bowling on the Clyde, the
proposed much broader and deeper Scottish Ship Canal should be diverted to
flow into the southern end of Loch Lomond. The loch, the British mainland's
largest stretch of inland water, could, it was suggested, provide a sheltered
base for northern operations.

A feasibility report was commissioned in 1889. Its findings were that
such a venture was practical. Access to the Clyde and the west coast of
Scotland would be via a link from Loch Lomond to Loch Long; the exit to
the Forth would be at South Alloa, with two locks at either end to raise ships
twenty-two feet above sea level. Encouraged by these recommendations, a
provisional Forth and Clyde Ship Canal Committee was appointed. A further
report by Glasgow engineers Crouch and Hogg in 1890 recommended a
more direct route from Grangemouth to Kilsyth, then on to Kirkintilloch,
Yoker and the Clyde.

Nothing came of this costly plan, and the completion of work on the
other ambitious scheme of the 1890s – the mighty cantilever Forth Railway
Bridge – cast even greater doubt on the future use of the river by the Royal
Navy. The reason for this was that the navy chiefs in London feared that in
time of war the bridge would be a natural target for enemy action. If it were

Fig. 4
The Firth of Forth was the scene of the surrender of the ships of the German Navy on 21 November 1918. Here ships of the Royal Navy's 5th Battle Squadron are seen steaming out to receive the ships of their defeated enemy.

Fig. 6

Opposite. The crew of the battleship HMS Barham stared out from the deck of their vessel as they strove to catch a first glimpse of the surrendered German ships.

Fig. 7

Top. At last the sailors of HMS Barham were rewarded with their first sighting of the leading vessel of the surrendered German fleet steaming over the horizon.

Fig. 8

Middle. The light cruiser HMS Cardiff had the honour of leading the first of the thirty-four surrendered vessels as they steamed from the North Sea, formerly known as the German Ocean, into the mouth of the Firth of Forth.

Fig. 9

Bottom.The battle-cruiser HMS Tiger was also present at the surrender of the German naval vessels. HMS Tiger was built by John Brown & Co. Ltd at Clydebank, where she was launched in 1914.

Fig. 12

A British airship, probably the R 23, flew high overhead as British battleships lead the way into the Firth of Forth at the surrender of the German navy on 21st November 1918. The warship sailing out in front is HMS Elizabeth.

Fig. 13

This third aerial view shows the surrendered German battleship Kaiser. She was built at Kiel in the Baltic in 1911 and a whole class of battleships was named after her. After being scuttled by her crew while she lay at anchor in Scapa Flow she was subsequently raised by Cox and Danks, and was then towed back south to the Forth, where she was broken up at Rosyth.

Fig. 14
The British airship NS8 kept watch over the long line of surrendered German naval vessels.

Fig. 15
The surrendered German battle-cruisers, Hindenburg, Moltke *and* Seydlitz *were photographed from the air as they sailed into the Firth of Forth. Years later, after they were scuttled by their crews while they lay at anchor in Scapa Flow, the hulls of all three were towed back to the Forth to be scrapped at Rosyth.*

Fig. 16
Below. The British White Ensign flown over the German flag indicated the surrender of this German vessel on 21 November 1918.

Fig. 17
Right. The surrendered battleship Kaiser is seen again in this aerial photograph.

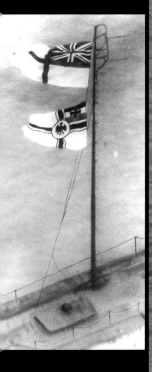

Fig. 18

Above. *The German battleships made a truly impressive sight as they steamed into the Firth of Forth to submit to surrender on 21 November 1918.*

Fig. 19

Right. *The interior of the cabin of the British airship R 23, from which many of the aerial views of the surrendered German ships were captured, was itself photographed in this unusual shot.*

Fig. 20

Above. *By sunset, late in the afternoon of 21 November, British destroyers had accompanied their defeated German counterparts to an anchorage off Inchkeith, the largest of the islands in the River Forth, situated between Leith and Kirkcaldy.*

Fig. 21

Left. *Rear Admiral Meurer stepped aboard the flagship of the Royal Navy's Fifth Battle Squadron to accept the terms of the surrender of his ships.*

Fig. 22

Rear Admiral Meurer was honoured by a guard of members of the flagship's crew as he walked along the deck of the British vessel, which only ten days earlier had still been at war with his country.

hit and at all badly damaged, vessels of the British fleet might easily be trapped upriver of the obstruction and thus be rendered inoperational.

Another major obstacle to the building of a Royal Naval Dockyard on the Forth was the outspoken opposition of First Sea Lord, Lord Fisher, to the entire proposal. In the end, however, he was overruled by Prime Minister Balfour and on 5 March 1903 it was announced in the House of Commons that the government intended to establish a naval base in Scotland, and that it was to be developed at a site on the Fife shore of the Forth near St Margaret's Hope, to the west of the ferry pier at North Queensferry.

It then took three years to finalise negotiations to purchase 1,182 acres of riverside estate from the Marquis of Linlithgow, whose stately home, Hopetoun House, was situated on the south shore of the Forth, directly opposite where the new naval dockyard was to be created near the site of Rosyth Castle.

The castle sat originally on a rock on the edge of the Forth and could only be reached by a causeway at low tide. Built in the sixteenth century, the three-storey tower is still in excellent condition. The ground- and first-floor rooms of the tower have vaulted ceilings, and all three floors are linked by narrow defensive spiral staircases. According to tradition, Rosyth Castle was a romantic hideaway for King Malcolm Canmore and his second wife, Margaret, but the royal assignations must have taken place in an earlier building because a stone slab above the entrance of the present one confirms that it was completed in 1561.

Another interesting tradition connected with Rosyth Castle is that the earlier building was the scene of an affray between the Lord of Tulliallan and the Abbot of Culross, the small port five miles further up the Forth on the Fife shore. Culross is carefully looked after by the National Trust for Scotland, whose first acquisition it was after its foundation in 1932. After a fierce quarrel over money due for the rent of some land, the abbot was slain. The laird, no doubt appalled by this tragic outcome, then rode off with his servants and sought refuge at Torphichen Preceptory, the Scottish headquarters of the Knights of the Order of St John of Jerusalem, seven miles inland from the southern shore of the river. The laird was given refuge, but only until he and his entourage could be provided with an armed escort to ensure their safe passage to Edinburgh, where they were tried by the High Court. There they were all found guilty of the murder of the abbot, but only the laird was sentenced to be executed; the court held that his servants were simply acting as good servants should in obeying the orders of their master and all were pardoned.

Other stories connected with Rosyth Castle link it with Oliver Cromwell. One claim is that Rosyth was his mother's birthplace, but this family connection certainly did not save it when it was amongst several castles, also including Blackness, which his troops attacked during their invasion of Scotland. The Cromwellian soldiers' attack on Roysth apparently resulted in some damage, as evinced by the date 1655 carved above the mullioned window on the east side, which shows where repairs took place.

The Barony of Rosyth was acquired by Sir David Stuart in 1435, and the castle remained in his hands until the start of the nineteenth century, when it was sold to Lord Rosebery of Dalmeny House, which is situated on the south shore of the forth between Queensferry and Cramond. Lord Rosebery sold the castle and the surrounding lands to the Marquis of Linlithgow, who eventually sold it to the Admiralty for the construction of the dockyard.

In 1906, as part of the forward planning for the new dockyard, it was also announced to the members of the House of Commons that the anchorage, which would be capable of accommodating all ships of the British fleet at all states of the tide, was to be known as St Margaret's Hope, while the dockyard was to be named Rosyth, after the existing castle. Although not mentioned at the time, Rosyth was an appropriate name, as it meant 'the landing place on the peninsula', which well described the site before construction commenced.

The decision to go ahead with the construction of Rosyth renewed debate

Dock I
from North Wall.

Fig. 23
Construction of Rosyth Dockyard.

This was the stage construction on Dock One had reached in the Autumn of 1913, less than a year before the outbreak of the First World War.

- Basin Sluices -
Nº 1 2 3 4 5

...de of work when "B" con
was substituted for "A".
- Nº 5 invert "B" concrete -
Date 9.1.'13

Position of
Sluice Shaft.

View looking N. showing loco-road
across Nº one. 82.

(Site of accident to L.M. Groves)
on 21/1/1914

Figs. 24 & 25

Construction of Rosyth Dockyard. The written comment on the bottom photograph refers to an accident which happened during the construction works.

about guaranteed access to the new base, and, with this in mind, a Royal Commission was set up to examine once again the feasibility of a Scottish ship canal which would provide alternative access from the west coast. In his evidence to the Commission, Vice-Admiral Sir Charles Campbell, speaking in favour, stressed that it should be regarded as, 'a Scottish battleship canal'. Influenced by his address to them, the commissioners requested that a plan which would satisfy the admiralty's requirements for naval use be drawn up. But, in the end, it concluded that 'while a ship canal through Loch Lomond would have some strategic value, it would not be sufficient to justify large-scale government expenditure on the project'.

Despite the report of the Royal Commission, the campaign for the new canal continued and, as the likelihood of hostilities in Europe increased, in 1912, no less a person than Winston Churchill, speaking as First Lord of the Admiralty, pronounced in favour of the idea.

Back in 1906, as plans for Rosyth moved slowly forward, one of the Royal Navy's existing links with the Forth had ended with the withdrawal from service and breaking up of the wooden-hulled sailing ship HMS *Caledonia*, which since 1891 had been moored off the Royal and Ancient Burgh of Queensferry as a floating training stablishment with 190 officers and men and 800 boy sailors.

In contrast to the disappearance of this historic vessel, the Forth caught one of its first glimpses of the Royal Navy's most modern deterrent when, the following year, the first submarine squadron (which had only been established in 1901) was ordered to prove if Rosyth could be adequately defended. To ascertain this, four of the new submarines, including C3 and C4, sailed north to the Forth and took part in a secret exercise, during which the former cruiser HMS *Thames* staged a mock attack on the future site of the dockyard at Rosyth.

The Admiralty was apparently satisfied with the outcome, and a few months later, in 1908, Robert McAlpine and Son were at last given the order to start work on the site by laying the necessary access roads. In February 1909, the contract for the construction of the dockyard itself was finally awarded to Easton Gibb, a Welsh firm from Newport.

By 1910 a branch railway line had been laid into the dockyard and a Pullman coach, used until then by the American showman Buffalo Bill during his British tours, was acquired for the use of distinguished visitors to the base. To begin with, however, there were few visitors and there was equally little for them to see. After 1912, there were more signs of progress, but, by the time of the declaration of the First World War in 1914, Rosyth Royal Naval Dockyard was still only two thirds complete and no part of it was

Fig. 26

Top. *According to tradition, the furthest upriver of the Forth islands, Inchgarvie, has been fortified since the reign of King Angus in the eighth century. During the First World War it took on a significant new strategic importance as it was the foundation for one of the massive cantilevers of the then comparatively new Forth Railway Bridge. It was therefore deemed of sufficient importance to warrant its own garrison. This view of the island is taken looking east down the Firth of Forth.*

Fig. 27

Bottom. *This gun was one of several mounted on Inchgarvie, below the Forth Railway Bridge, during the First World War. Notice how it was constructed to pivot through 360 degrees. Ammunition is seen piled in the foreground and ships of the fleet are glimpsed in the background.*

capable of receiving any ships. The start of hostilities with Germany brought a flurry of activity and, shortly afterwards, the tidal basin was flooded. Ten months later, in June 1915, King George V travelled north by train to Fife to perform the official opening ceremony. But it was not until March of the following year that the dockyard was fully operational, and by then the war was half over.

The increased operational importance of the Firth of Forth after the creation of Rosyth did, however, from the outset of hostilities, result in an increase in the defences on the river. According to tradition, the furthest upriver of the Forth's islands, Inchgarvie, named after the shoals of young herring which used to be plentiful in this part of the river, had in fact been fortified since the time of King Angus in the eighth century. More modern fortifications had been added at the time of the Napoleonic Wars, but, now that it formed the base for one of the cantilevers of the vital transport link, the Forth Rail Bridge, it was judged prudent to provide it with a gun battery.

The existing gun emplacements on the largest of the islands, Inchkeith, lying between Leith and Kirkcaldy, were also brought back into use and new ones were built on the smaller island of Inchcolm, which lies off the Fife shore opposite Aberdour. To make Inchcolm a more efficient base, men of the 576 Cornwall Works Company of the Royal Engineers were sent to the island in 1916. Between then and the following year, they excavated a tunnel through the rocky hillside in order to make it easier to supply the gun emplacements at the eastern end of the island with ammunition. The brick-lined tunnel is still in good repair and a plaque records the details of its construction. The soldiers of the island garrison were housed in the remains of the island's famous Augustine abbey, which were converted into billets. The holes in the walls of the refectory where bunk beds were installed to make a dormitory can still be seen. Although none of the guns installed on Inchcolm now remain, visitors to the island can still explore the remains of the gun emplacements, where metal tracks are still visible. These enabled the four-point-seven- and four-inch guns to be pivoted round to meet an attack from any direction. The smaller circular tracks were installed for the twelve-pounders, pompoms and anti-aircraft guns with which the island was also defended.

From where these tracks are situated, the lower path leads round to the south-east side of the island, where the Second World War searchlight battery is still comparatively intact. Its powerful lamps could probe the night sky for enemy raiders, as they did on the nights of 13 and 14 March 1941, when German bombers used the Forth as a flight path to guide them across central Scotland to launch their deadly blitz on Clydebank. The searchlights could

Fig. 28

Top. *Inchkeith, the largest island in the Firth of Forth, lying between Leith and Kirkcaldy, was fortified in the Middle Ages and was again garrisoned and strongly defended during both World Wars. As well as army barracks and fortifications on the island, anti-submarine boom defences can be seen offshore.*

Fig. 29

Bottom. *The harbour and barracks erected by the army are seen in this aerial view of Inchkeith. Inchkeith is privately owned and members of the public are not allowed ashore.*

Fig. 30

Top. *Below the mighty cantilever span of the Forth Railway Bridge, gunners of the artillery garrison which manned Inchgarvie throughout the First World War are seen rowing ashore to enjoy a few hours of rest and relaxation in the pubs and cafés of Queensferry, before returning to their island outpost. Although thousands of train travellers passed right above their heads every day throughout the four years of the hostilities, Inchgarvie was a lonely outpost for the soldiers who served there.*

Fig. 31

Bottom. *A gunner mans his post on Inchgarvie during the First World War, with the span of the Forth Railway Bridge looming in the background.*

Fig. 32

Four of the officers who manned the defences on Inchgarvie found time to pose for the photographer on the island's rock-strewn shore.

also, if necessary, illuminate the long boom supporting the anti-submarine net, which protected the Firth from underwater attack at this point. Electrical power was produced by a generator whose house can also still be seen. Inchcolm is nowadays in the care of Historic Scotland, which has plans, as part of its Project Defence scheme, to protect these First and Second World War military remains, and display them in a more meaningful way to the island's many summer visitors.

Inchcolm is easily reached either by the Forth pleasure vessel, *Maid of the Forth*, which sails from the Hawes pier at Queensferry and from Town Pier at North Queensferry on the opposite shore, or by chartering a boat at Aberdour harbour. The other Forth islands, Inchkeith, Inchgarvie and Inchmickery, however, are not open to the public. Inchmickery served an unusual function during the First World War, when dummy funnels and masts were erected on it to capitalise on its boat-like silhouette and thus try to encourage the Germans to waste their ammunition by attacking it. Ever since, it has been nicknamed 'Battleship Island'.

The declaration of war in August 1914 had an immediate effect on shipping on the Forth, as the Admiralty swiftly imposed restrictions. Two armed naval inspection vessels took up position off Inchkeith, and captains of merchant vessels were instructed that they must report to them upon their arrival in the firth, which must be during the hours of daylight. Arrivals and departures were prohibited in foggy conditions, and all vessels sailing out of the river were warned that they must do so before nightfall, as the river's lighthouses were put out of action. Pilotage was made compulsory for all but the smallest ships and all were banned from sending radio messages. Any ships failing to obey these regulations were informed that they were liable to be fired at.

There were, in any case, far fewer shipping movements than normal, as Leith owners such as Currie Line and George Gibson Company suspended their regular sailings to the continent for fear of mines. The only German vessels in the port were two small cargo steamers, the *Otto* and the *Adolf*, which were seized as prizes and detained in the West Old Dock. They were joined within days by the *Naute*, the *Mowe*, and the schooner *Fidro*, which were seized at sea and escorted into port.

ADMIRALTY REQUISITIONS
PORTS OF GRANGEMOUTH AND BO'NESS

Both Grangemouth and Bo'ness docks were requisitioned by the Admiralty. The closure at Grangemouth came in two stages, the first of which was implemented on what local shipping firms regarded as a very unlucky Friday, 13 November. This closure still permitted very limited commercial traffic, but the second, on Wednesday 25 November, banned all merchant shipping for the duration of the hostilities. From then on, Grangemouth was known officially as HMS *Rameses*. It was commanded by Admiral L. Clinton Baker, who, with his large staff, occupied the three-storey-high red sandstone Baltic Buildings in Lumley Street as his headquarters. Other buildings in the town were also requisitioned to provide barracks for the sailors, a large number of whom were accommodated in a converted granary, paint store and sail-maker's loft in Carron Street. The WRNS took up residence in the YMCA building in Abbotsgrange Road, which, over fifty years later, still bore the sign 'HMS *Rameses*' above its entrance.

Many of the naval personnel were employed at the mine-manufacturing works and training school which was established in a series of long low sheds

Fig. 33

Top. *Camouflage paint was used during the war to try to make the hulls of naval vessels more difficult for the enemy to spot when they were at sea. This view, taken during the years when the port of Grangemouth was requisitioned by the Admiralty for the exclusive use of the Royal Navy, shows the converted passenger vessel* Princess Margaret *in her dangerous role as a minelayer. Above the quay-side shed a mine can be seen being loaded aboard by crane.*

Fig. 34

Bottom. *The use of camouflage is again seen in this photograph of the converted British mailsteamer* Wahine, *in her wartime role as a minelayer, lying alongside in the docks at Grangemouth. In peacetime the* Wahine, *as her Maori name indicated, plied between Great Britain and New Zealand.*

Fig. 35

The mine-layers Princess
Margaret *and* Wahine,
*seen in the previous two
pictures, are joined by
HMS* Angora *in this
further photograph of the
Grangemouth Mine-laying
Base.*

Fig. 36

*The size and extent of the
base and training school at
Grangemouth are seen
clearly in this photograph,
which also shows some of
the naval officers walking
to a staff car. The single-
storey construction of the
long low sheds which
made up the mine-laying
base was deliberate to try
to minimise damage and
casualties in the event of
an explosion during the
manufacture of the mines.*

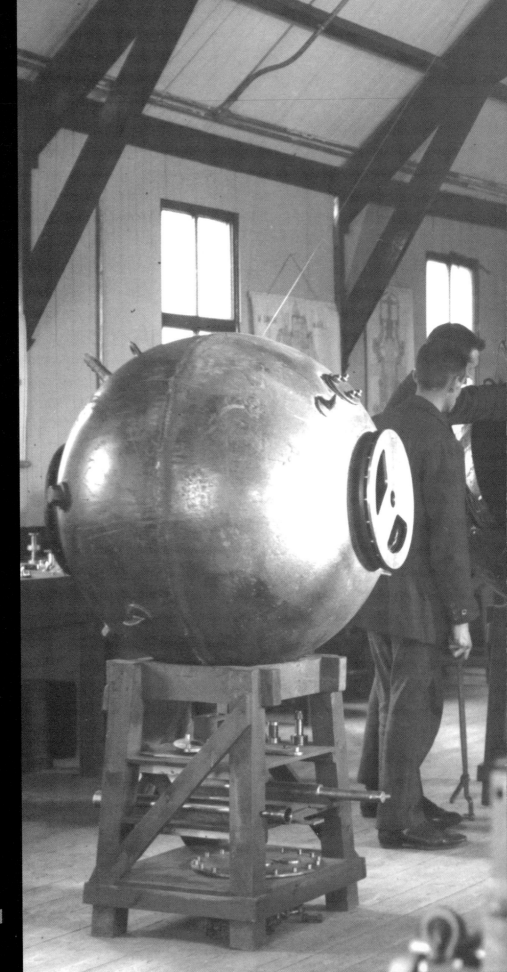

Fig. 37
To try to prevent accidents
in the course of the
highly-dangerous process
of producing mines, the
Grangemouth base
operated a training
school. This photograph
was taken during one of
the lectures held there.

Fig. 38

Top. *Civilian workers as well as naval personnel were employed at Grangemouth. Here several of them are seen at work in one of the sheds testing the connection of a mine.*

Fig. 39

Bottom. *Before they were loaded on to the mine-layers moored alongside in Grangemouth docks, the mines were all carefully checked by immersing them in a test-tank to detect water leakage.*

Fig. 40

Opposite. *Women who were used to sewing were found to be particularly good at working on the intricate process of constructing the deadly explosive mines.*

Fig. 41
The serried ranks of mines
stored at Grangemouth are
a grim reminder of the
extent to which mines were
used by both sides during
the four years of hostilities.

Fig. 42

This mine was used for instructional purposes in the training school.

within the docks. The coal chutes at the docks were also used for bunkering a wide variety of naval vessels, while the Admiralty also took over the recently-established British Petroleum Company's oil installation as an oil-fuelling depot. Barges were hurriedly converted to transport oil on the Forth and Clyde Canal, and in them large quantities of fuel were shipped from Bowling on the river Clyde across Central Scotland to Grangemouth, where a large tank farm was developed to ensure a plentiful supply for the ships of the fleet. The maintenance of this oil supply was considered so vital that plans were made to establish an oil pipeline from Old Kilpatrick near Bowling to Grangemouth, to replace the canal barges. This was eventually built by an American government pipe-laying team, but was not completed and in use until 1 November 1918, only ten days before the Armistice was signed.

Interestingly, the British Petroleum Company, from which the Grangemouth oil depot was requisitioned by the Admiralty, was not the present well-known company of that name and, despite its title, was actually German-owned. It was never returned to its owners: after the end of the First World War, it was acquired from the custodian of enemy property by the Anglo-Persian Oil Company, which later merged with Scottish Oils Ltd, and eventually became the present British Petroleum Company. Although the original pre-war British Petroleum Company was thus taken over, it is also interesting to note that the oil-storage tanks utilised by the Royal Navy were not handed over as part of the war reparations, but were retained by the Admiralty as a facility until well into the 1960s.

Another of the Stirlingshire town's industries which was completely absorbed by the war effort was the Grangemouth Dockyard Company Ltd, at whose premises on the River Carron many naval vessels were repaired. The dockyard became so busy that the adjoining Carron Wharf was also taken over to ease the congestion. Additional dry-docking facilities were made available by utilising the locks at the dock gates of the town's Old and Carron Docks, which had not been used as entrances to the port since 1882 and 1906 respectively.

Throughout the war, Grangemouth was considered such a vital naval base that it was constantly garrisoned, first by a battalion of the Scottish Rifles and thereafter by the Black Watch and the Argyll and Sutherland Highlanders. A government-recruited Marine Labour Corps of 200 men was also based in the town to provide extra labour at the docks. From the outset of the hostilities the Admiralty also began to requisition many small vessels on the Forth for naval use, ranging from tugs to fishing boats.

Taking over both Grangemouth and Bo'ness meant that the Admiralty had virtually exclusive use of the upper Forth, while still permitting controlled commercial traffic to operate further down the firth. However, although Leith was not officially closed to merchant shipping, the Royal Navy's presence was increasingly felt as it took over larger areas of the docks and quayside buildings, including several warehouses. Although this led to considerable disruption, commercial necessity drove the port's ship-owners to get their vessels back to sea on voyages to neutral continental countries, despite the risks involved. Commercial ships might suffer damage from mines or attacks from submarines, the new underwater menace of the First World War, and a weapon which truly allowed the Germans to be the enemy at the door.

Just how literally this was true was proved on 5 September 1914, when the cruiser HMS *Pathfinder* became the first British naval vessel to be sunk by a torpedo fired by a U-boat; she was hit as she sailed to the south-east of the Isle of May at the entrance to the Forth. The *Shipwreck Index of the British Isles* by Richard and Bridget Larn states that the torpedo was launched by *U21* and scored a direct hit on the *Pathfinder*'s forward ammunition magazine. There was a deafening explosion, and, as the water rushed in, *Pathfinder* sank in only four minutes, with the loss of all but nine of her ship's company.

Less than two months later, the first Merchant Navy vessel with Forth connections became a casualty of the war: the Leith-registered general cargo vessel, *Glitra*, belonging to Salvesen Line, was lost to enemy action. She was on passage from Grangemouth, only days before that port was closed, across the North Sea to Stavanger in Norway, when she was stopped by a U-boat on 30 October. The U-boat captain ordered her master and crew to take to the lifeboats. Sailors from the U-boat then boarded the *Glitra* and opened her sluices. Then, as the Leith vessel sank low in the water, the U-boat finished the vessel off with a round of shells, before submerging again to lie in wait for her next prey.

Five days later, on 3 November, the armed patrol trawler *Ivanhoe*, which had been requisitioned by the Admiralty, hit the Black Rock near Leith while laying mines and sank. The navy suffered a second self-inflicted disaster the following month when, on 27 December, as thick winter fog blanketed the estuary, the destroyer HMS *Success* ran aground on the treacherous Cambo Sands off Kingsbarns on the Fife shore of the firth.

The following spring, on 10 March 1915, the German submarine *U12* launched an attack on several naval trawlers off the Isle of May. The German U-boat was chased by three Royal Navy destroyers; she tried to evade them but was rammed and sunk by one of the Royal Navy ships, HMS *Ariel*.

Six weeks later, on 28 April, the North Shields trawler *Lilydale* was peacefully fishing off St Abbs Head, close to the mouth of the firth, when a German U-boat suddenly surfaced almost alongside and captured her. Her crew were given time to safely abandon ship before she was sunk. This gentlemanly conduct still prevailed when, on 10 August, in the same waters the trawler *Utopia* was attacked and sunk by another enemy U-boat.

All of the casualties of 1915 were not necessarily inflicted by the Germans: on 18 November the Norwegian sailing schooner *Noas* sank off the Isle of May after being badly damaged in a collision which the *Shipwreck Index* simply lists was 'with an unidentified Royal Navy cruiser'.

Enemy action was not confined to attacks on shipping, but also included the shelling of several east-coast towns, including Scarborough and Hartlepool. These raids shocked the nation and caused grave concern at the Admiralty, where Lord Jellicoe expressed the view that stationing the British fleet at Scapa Flow meant it was too far away to intercept effectively the German High Seas Fleet as it harried English coastal towns.

The problem with moving the Royal Navy further south from Scapa Flow in the Northern Isles to the Forth was one of security. It was feared that the Navy's ships could well be trapped in the Forth by the enemy. The Germans could lay mines, or launch a Zeppelin bombing raid (as they later did on Edinburgh), to demolish the Forth Bridge, thus creating a barrier across the river which would be difficult and time-consuming to clear. On 20 November 1914, however, it was finally decided to detach the 3rd Battle Squadron from the Channel Fleet and to base it, together with the 3rd Cruiser Squadron, at the still-incomplete Rosyth. The Battle Squadron consisted of eight ships of King Edward VII class; the Cruiser Squadron was made up of four ships of the County class. These battleships and cruisers were provided with escort destroyers as defensive support.

There was, however, always the fear that German-laid minefields might endanger all of these vessels. In 1916 Lord Jellicoe held a meeting at Rosyth, at which he proposed that a scheme of submarine obstructions be put in place to safeguard British naval vessels. Work began immediately on the underwater defences, and practices were completed by 16 December, although all of the obstructions were not successfully in place until July 1917. Jellicoe himself never saw his grand scheme in place. On 27 July 1916, upon his return to Rosyth aboard his flagship, the battleship HMS *Iron Duke*, he found Prime Minister Balfour waiting for him on the quayside. At

the meeting which subsequently took place on board, he was ordered to return to London to take charge of affairs at the Admiralty. He was succeeded as Commander of the Grand Fleet by Admiral David Beatty.

Meanwhile, on 2 April 1916, the danger of mines was illustrated when the SS *Sabbia*, which had been requisitioned by the Admiralty as a collier, was blown up off Dunbar. Later that same day a similar fate overtook another small vessel, also on Admiralty collier service, *CT29*, which was blown out of the sea in these same waters. The Germans, however, also suffered losses, perhaps because of their own mines. On 7 July, the submarine *U77* sank mysteriously off St. Abbs Head the same East Lothian holiday resort. There were no survivors of this tragedy. On 5 November, the Admiralty-requisitioned trawler *Knot* was lost when she grounded off Fife Ness at the mouth of the firth.

The next enemy action in the Forth came early the following year, when, on 7 February 1917, the trawler *Shakespeare* was captured by a patrolling U-boat. Although the German High Command had by this time ordered U-boat commanders to sink on sight, the crew of the *Shakespeare* were given time to abandon ship before she was sunk. The same thing happened later the same day when the cargo ship, SS *Boyne Castle* was attacked and sunk of St Abbs Head, but whether same U-boat was responsible for two sinkings is not known.

It is known, however, that it was *U22* which stopped and sank the SS *Bellax* off the Isle of May three days later, on 10 February. At the start of the following month, a similar fate awaited the *Tilly Cobthe* as she sailed off St Abbs Head; two days later the SS *Ring* was also hit by a torpedo there and subsequently sank. That same day, on the opposite shore of the Forth, the trawler *Northumbria*, which had been requisitioned by the Admiralty, hit a mine off Fife Ness and sank. Another Admiralty-requisitioned fishing boat, the drifter *Campania II*, also sank two days later and, although the cause of her loss was never officially confirmed, it is thought that she hit a mine. The toll of casualties in the Forth continued later that month when, on 24 March, the German submarine *UC77* sank the Norwegian cargo vessel SS *Grenmar*. Four days later, while on the same patrol, the *UC77* claimed a second kill when she successfully chased and torpedoed the Norwegian cargo vessel SS *Tizona*.

There was then a lull in enemy action in the Forth until 13 April, when the *Stork* was sunk by a U-boat, followed on 18 April by two trawlers, the *John S. Boyle* and the *Rameses*, which were probably sunk by the same U-boat. One of the worst days of the war for enemy action in the river was 20 April, which saw the loss of three vessels within twenty-four hours. The

Fig. 43
Admiral Sir David Beatty GCB, KCVO, DSC, photographed on the deck of his flagship at Rosyth shortly after his appointment in the summer of 1916. He proved a very popular choice with both officers and crew.

trawler *Othonna*, which had been requisitioned by the Admiralty as an
armed patrol vessel, hit a mine and sank off Fife Ness, while the SS
Ballochbuie and the Norwegian-owned SS *Ringholm* were torpedoed. The
latter sank off St Abbs Head after being chased by *UC41*. Another
Scandinavian casualty three days later was the Danish-owned SS *Baron
Stjernblad*, which was torpedoed then shelled by *UC44*. Later the same day
UC44 also sank the SS *Auriac* off Eyemouth. She completed a busy day's
work when she sank the Danish cargo vessel SS *Scot* off St Abbs Head.

On 5 May, *U77* was back in action sinking the SS *Odense* from Denmark
off St Abbs Head. Four days later, also off St Abbs, the Peterhead trawler
Kitty was attacked by a U-boat. The U-boat then surfaced and took aboard
the skipper and first engineer of the *Kitty* as prisoners. The remainder of the
crew were allowed to launch the lifeboat before the *Kitty* was shelled and
sunk.

On 6 June the *U77* was back in the mouth of the Forth and this time her
victim was the Danish-registered cargo vessel SS *Harald Klitgaard*, which was
torpedoed off St Abbs Head. July passed without incident, but on 22 August
the trawler *Sophron*, which had been requisitioned by the Admiralty and was
operating as an armed patrol mine sweeper, went down off Fife Ness when
she herself hit a mine. On 3 January 1918 the whaling ship *Blackwhale*,
which had been requisitioned by the Admiralty, also sank in the river after
hitting a mine.

A famous feature of British naval tactics during the First World War was
the deployment of what became known as Q-ships. These were innocuous-
looking merchant vessels which lured enemy vessels to attack them. As soon
as the enemy were within range, the bulkheads on the Q-ships were removed,
revealing cunningly-concealed artillery, with which they opened fire. These
decoy vessels were based both at Leith and Grangemouth. Their most famous
captain was Commander Campbell, who became very much a local hero for
his daring exploits at this time. On 28 January, two of the Q-ships from
Leith saw action in the mouth of the Forth: the converted trawlers HMS *W.S.
Bailey* and HMS *Fort George*. While on patrol together off the Isle of May
they detected the sounds of an enemy submarine and pursued. The chase
went on for one and a half hours until the crew of the *W.S. Bailey* spotted
two periscopes breaking the surface only twenty yards astern of their ship.
The periscopes disappeared, but the *W.S. Bailey* went swiftly astern and
dropped a single depth-charge. It scored a direct hit on the U-boat and within
minutes the surface of the water was littered with debris and oil from the
stricken German vessel.

After this triumph for the British navy, tragedy struck only three days later, when there occurred the incident which became known as the Battle of the May Island. A month earlier, the 12th and 13th Submarine Squadrons had been repositioned from Scapa Flow to Rosyth. These two squadrons were both equipped with the Royal Navy's most modern vessels – K class submarines. Built by Vickers of Barrow-in-Furness in 1916 and 1917, the K class submarines were the largest underwater craft then in existence. They were powered while on the surface by steam turbines, which meant that they required funnels. These had to be lowered and stowed before the submarines could submerge.

Late in the afternoon of 31 January, as dusk settled over the river, nine of these strange-looking submarines set to sea from Rosyth to accompany Admiral Beatty's fleet on exercise in the North Sea. In flotilla they sailed below the Forth Bridge and, as darkness fell, on down the firth. Off the May Island they encountered a group of mine-sweepers, which, unaware of the exercise, sailed straight across the path of the sea-going fleet. Trying to take avoiding action in the pitch darkness, *K22* hit *K14*, slicing off her bows. The battle-cruiser HMS *Inflexible* then collided with the already-damaged bow of *K22*. The radio silence which had been imposed during the exercise was then broken and all vessels were ordered to display their navigation lights. But no message was transmitted to warn the oncoming ships that several of the vessels in the van of the fleet had by then changed course and were in the midst of turning. As a result, the cruiser HMS *Fearless* hit *K17*. Her crew managed to escape before she sank, but much worse was to follow. Her sister vessels *K3* and *K4* both stopped and this resulted in the latter being hit by *K6*, which almost sliced her in half. Locked together, the two submarines began to sink quickly and it was only by going astern that *K6* managed to avoid being drawn under as *K4* rolled over and sank, drowning all members of her ship's company. More lives were lost as the following surface-vessels ploughed into the sailors from the other damaged submarines, who were struggling in the water. The final death toll reached 100. The wrecks of *K4* and *K17* have never been raised and still lie about fifty-five metres down on the sea bed off the Isle of May as a memorial to this First World War disaster.

The casualties of war around the Isle of May continued to mount when, two months later, on 3 March, the trawler *Columba*, which had been hired by the Admiralty as a boom defence vessel, hit a mine and sank. By this time *UB62* was on patrol in the Forth estuary; on 12 March she made her first

Fig. 44

K-class submarines were the largest and most powerful in the British navy during the First World War. Here HM Submarine K3 is seen alongside a battleship at Rosyth . This view, taken from the battleship, looking towards the bows of the submarine, clearly shows the funnels which her steam turbines necessitated, and which had to be carefully battened down before every dive. The deck-mounted guns, aft of the two funnels and for'ard of the vessel's conning tower, are a reminder that during the First World War submarine warfare was conducted as much on the surface as underwater. It was a flotilla of submarines of this class which was involved in the tragic incident which became known as the Battle of the May Island in January 1918.

Fig. 45

Top. *With smoke
billowing from her two
funnels, K3 is seen at sea,
travelling at high speed
with waves crashing
across her bows.*

Fig. 46

Bottom. *A fine view of
HM Submarine K16 on
the surface in calm waters.
During the First World
War this class of vessel
was considered one of the
Royal Navy's most
powerful new weapons.*

Fig. 47

Opposite. *HM Submarine
K8 is pictured in this
photograph as a torpedo
was hoisted carefully on
board.*

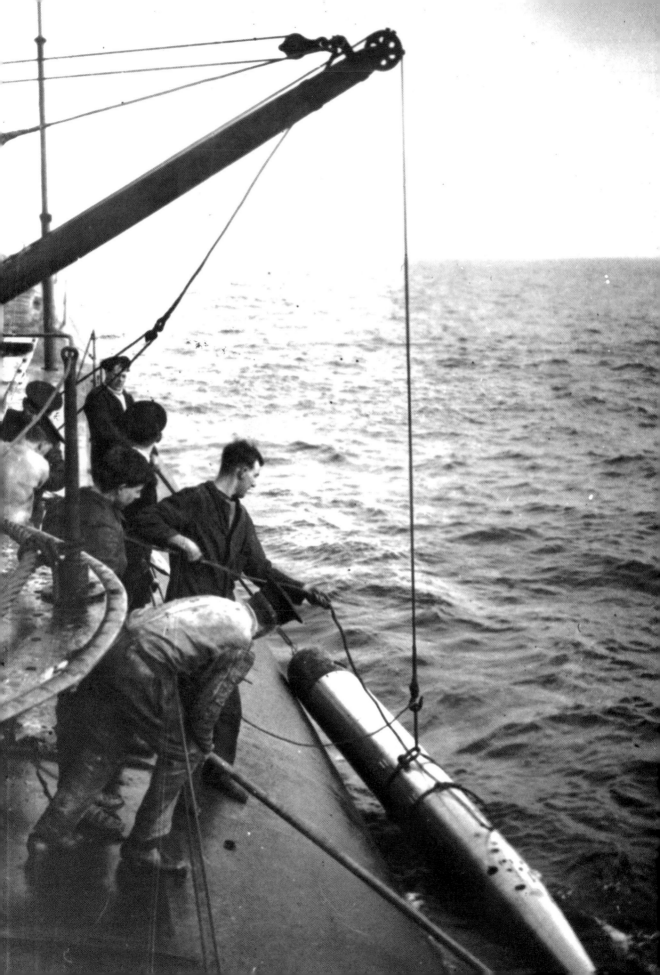

Fig. 48

Top. A tug escorts HMS Zealandia into the Royal Naval dockyard at Rosyth during the First World War.

Fig. 49

Bottom. HMS Crescent entering one of the docks at Rosyth.

kills when she torpedoed the Swedish-registered cargo vessel, *SS Oswin* and, a week later, the British- registered cargo vessel SS *Burnstone*.

The fishing drifter *Sunbeam* sank off Inchcolm Island on 16 April after being in collision with an unknown vessel, and on 24 April the trawler *Emley*, which had been requisitioned by the Admiralty, sank off the May Island when she hit a mine.

The war was in its closing stages when, on 2 November, the trawler *Charles Hammond*, which had been requisitioned by the Admiralty, was in a collision in the river with the destroyer HMS *Marksman*, and subsequently sank.

SINKING OF HMS *CAMPANIA*

By this point in the hostilities many of the ships of the British Grand Fleet were already laid up in Burntisland Bay. Amongst them was the former Cunard luxury liner and holder of the Blue Riband trophy for the fastest crossing of the Atlantic, the *Campania*.

When the people of Edinburgh and Dundee awoke on the morning of Saturday 6 November 1918 and unfolded the weekend issues of their *Scotsman*s and *Courier*s, they found their tightly-packed columns full of news. After four years of war, victory was at last only days away. Sailors of the German navy had mutinied at Kiel in the Baltic.

There was, however, not one single word in either paper about the biggest news story which had broken within their own circulation areas the previous day. The war censors had ensured there was no mention that carelessness had sunk the Royal Navy aircraft carrier HMS *Campania* off Burntisland in the Firth of Forth, within sight of the shore.

How the *Campania* came to be there as part of the British navy is an interesting story. The 12,950-ton liner was built on the Clyde by the Fairfield Engineering Company, not as an aircraft carrier, but as the latest luxury liner to join the Cunard fleet. Like all Cunard liners of the period, her name ended distinctively in the letters '-ia'. Together with her sister ship *Lucania*, also built by Fairfields, she was to revolutionise transatlantic travel, both because of her speed and her luxurious fittings, unsurpassed in her period.

After *Campania*'s launch at Govan on 8 September 1892, however, Cunard were not happy with their new vessel; speed trials off the Isle of Arran revealed excessive vibration. *Campania* was Cunard's first twin-screw vessel, and the two huge propellers were deemed to be the source of the problem. For a time, Cunard threatened to sue Fairfields, but after the pitch

Fig. 50

The 12,950-ton Cunard liner Campania *sailing down the River Clyde on her maiden voyage in 1893. At the start of the First World War she was about to be sent to the breakers because her coal-fired boilers were proving too costly to run, but the speed which they could achieve and her long sleek length persuaded the Admiralty to purchase her for conversion into the world's first aircraft carrier.*

of the propeller blades was changed the vibration was greatly reduced.

After a delay of seven months, SS *Campania* entered service on 22 April 1893. By the time she sailed on her maiden voyage the shaking was much reduced and, in any case, was really only felt by the 1,000 emigrants huddled together in steerage class (so called because it was situated in the stern of the ship, where her German-designed rudder and the propellers were situated). Meanwhile, her 600 pampered guests in first class and 400 passengers in the almost equally comfortable second class accommodation situated for'ard and amidships, never noticed the problem, even when the *Campania*'s captain ordered her full cruising speed of twenty-two knots. As they disembarked in the United States they were so full of praise for the delightfully comfortable crossing, which they had so much enjoyed, that on the return east-bound trip to Britain, her master was encouraged to urge an extra knot from *Campania*'s two 15,000 horsepower triple-expansion steam engines. She set a transatlantic record time of five days, seventeen hours and twenty-seven minutes, arriving home the proud holder of the coveted Blue Riband.

Campania was the pride of the Cunard fleet and the company's literature boasted of her special features: to ensure power, two enormous red funnels, each almost twenty feet in diameter and rising an impressive 130 feet from keel to rim; her perfectly designed and elegant razor-sharp bow to ensure speed; her twenty lifeboats to ensure safety. Along with *Lucania*, which entered service later the same year, *Campania* put Cunard well ahead of all of its British and continental rivals on the North Atlantic route, as the

nineteenth century drew to a close.

Throughout the first decade of the new century, *Campania* continued as the racehorse of the Atlantic fleet, but by 1910 Cunard were becoming concerned about the growing expense of operating her. The 100 furnaces required to heat *Campania*'s thirteen boilers ate up over twenty tons of coal an hour, a huge 500 tons of coal every day she was at sea. As her engines grew older, they were becoming ever more expensive to fuel.

So in 1914 Cunard decided to sell *Campania* to the breakers. The outbreak of hostilities soon afterwards rescued her from the scrap-yard; the Admiralty, desperately seeking a ship to convert into a new-fangled aircraft carrier, decided that she would be the ideal vessel. The reasons for her being chosen were her sleek, streamlined length and her still impressive speed. Now that Great Britain was at war, the cost of the coal and the wages of the 180 firemen and stokers required to achieve that speed no longer mattered! Up until the outbreak of the First World War, pioneering efforts to utilise the newly available air power in naval warfare had depended on seaplanes, which both took off and landed on water. Now the Lords of the Admiralty were determined to gain the advantage by launching planes from ships, and for that to succeed the speed of the vessel was all-important.

After *Campania* was purchased by the Royal Navy on 27 November 1914, it took almost eight months to refit her as one of the world's first aircraft carriers, complete with a 168-foot-long wooden flight deck stretching all the way from her bridge to her bows. At last, on 8 August 1915, all was

Fig. 51

As HMS Campania *the Royal Navy's earliest aircraft carrier at first retained both of her funnels, seen here rising above her camouflage-painted hull. Later the forward funnel was removed and replaced by two narrow smoke stacks, one on either side of her deck, in order to allow her wooden runway to be extended. In this photograph, the wooden runway can be seen stretching from her bridge to her bows.*

Fig. 53

*The Campania sank
swiftly after being
involved in a series of
collisions with other naval
vessels, but all of her
skeleton maintenance crew
were rescued by lifeboats
lowered by the
surrounding ships.*

ready for the first trial of a ship-borne take-off. *Campania*'s captain ordered
her to sail straight into the wind and rang down to the engine room for her
to increase her speed to her maximum twenty-three knots. As the now 23-
year-old former Atlantic liner surged forward, the pilot of the Sopworth Baby
seaplane on her flight deck throttled back and thundered along the planks of
her runway to make a first successful take-off. Triumphantly he circled the
ship, and dipped his wings in salute to the bridge, before touching down in
the water on the new aircraft carrier's lee side and being hoisted safely back
on board.

Despite this success, it was decided that *Campania*'s flight deck was definitely too short for operational use and so she was ordered back to port for further drastic modifications. These involved removing her forward funnel and replacing it with two narrow smoke-pipes on either side of the runway, now extended to 200 feet long. The work was completed by the end of April 1916 and *Campania* was ordered to sail with all speed to the Orkneys to rejoin the Grand Fleet at Scapa Flow.

It was then that her luck began to run out. Despite the long light evenings at the end of May in the Orkneys, *Campania*'s captain missed the final signal to set sail to challenge the German navy at the Battle of Jutland. And in the brief darkness of the northern night, he further failed to see that the rest of the British Grand Fleet had set sail from the anchorage at Scapa Flow. By the time dawn broke about two hours later, when the mistake became painfully obvious, the other ships of the fleet were over forty miles out into the North Sea.

Campania set to sea as soon as possible and, with her superior speed, would have caught up with the other vessels of the Grand Fleet in time to play her part in the vital battle. But Admiral Jellicoe doubted that she could arrive in time and ordered her back to Scapa Flow, thus robbing the Royal Navy of air reconnaissance in the ensuing fray. Her ill-luck continued, when, two months later, in August, essential repairs prevented her from taking part in the next attack on the German fleet. Despite these setbacks, in 1917 *Campania* was equipped with specially-built two-seater Fairey F 16s. They proved very successful as spotter planes and were named 'Campanias', after their mother ship.

For the final two years of the war *Campania* was only kept at sea with great difficulty, because of problems with her engines. When, in October 1918, as the war drew to a close, she anchored in the Forth off Burntisland with the rest of the Grand Fleet, it was decided she had little part left to play in the hostilities and her ship's company of 374 was reduced to a skeleton maintenance crew. They alone were aboard on 5 November 1918, when the weather suddenly began to change. With only one of her thirteen boilers operational to provide auxiliary power, the crew could do little as the wind from the south-west steadily increased to gale force.

As the full force of the gale caught *Campania*'s long hull, she dragged her anchor and was swept astern. With her crewmen looking on in helpless horror, she collided amidships with the famous battleship HMS *Royal Oak*. The tremendous impact caused *Campania*'s one boiler, which had steam up, to explode with a bang well fitted to the Guy Fawkes Day of the accident; it shook the whole of Burntisland.

As local people rushed to the shore to see what had happened, they saw that *Campania* was sinking, but, before she did so, the gale-force winds whipped her into another collision, this time with the battlecruiser HMS *Glorious*. The latter survived and, ironically, after the end of the war was converted into an aircraft carrier to replace the ill fated *Campania*.

After ramming *Glorious*, some reports say, *Campania* continued out of control to collide with another battleship, HMS *Revenge*, but this is not confirmed, and, in any case, she was by then so badly damaged that she began to go down. As she sank lower and lower, stern first, into the waters of the Forth, all of her maintenance crew were rescued by lifeboats from other ships of the Grand Fleet. Soon only her grey-painted funnel, which had once towered so proudly in its livery of Cunard red, and the two grey smoke-stacks which had replaced her other funnel, remained sticking out of the sea off Burntisland.

The loss of the *Campania* through such carelessness was a great embarrassment to the Royal Navy. It soon took advantage of the hazard her funnel and smoke-stacks posed to shipping entering and leaving the docks at Burntisland and blew them up as part of an exercise. According to Admiralty charts, *Campania*'s long hull lies broken in two on the bed of the Forth. But according to Colin Aston, the master of the Forth passenger cruise vessel *Maid of the Forth* and a keen diver, although her decks have collapsed, the once-proud Blue Riband holder is still intact.

[2]

THE INTER-WAR YEARS

The end of hostilities with the signing of the armistice on 11 November 1918 had major effects on the Royal Naval Dockyard at Rosyth. During the war this controversial northern base had more than proved its worth, logging dockings of seventy-eight capital ships, including super dreadnoughts, dreadnoughts and battle-cruisers, eighty-two light cruisers, and thirty-seven small craft, many of which had successfully undergone repairs or refits. With the return to peace, however, there was a major reduction in work and there were many payoffs. In 1921 those who remained were put on short time and, despite an assurance the following year that the government would provide sufficient work to occupy a minimum of 3,000 men, in 1923 it was announced that the yard was to be placed on a care and maintenance basis.

Ironically, the saviour of Rosyth turned out to be the ships of the German fleet. Deliberately scuttled by their crews where they lay at anchor in the vast natural harbour of Scapa Flow, they provided a rich trawl of salvage opportunities, and many of them met their end at Rosyth. The first of the German ships to be raised in 1925 were the destroyers, and ten of them were made sufficiently seaworthy to make the long voyage south to the Forth to be broken up.

The following year, the Rosyth Shipbreaking Company also purchased a large former German floating dock, whose scrapping provided additional work for the yard. This was followed in September of that year by the purchase of two Royal Navy submarines, *K12* and *K9*. Work on breaking them up began at Rosyth, but the remains of their hulls were later towed the short distance upriver on the same side of the Forth to the small harbour at Charlestown to be finished off. This was done in order to create space at Rosyth for the breaking up of HMS *Boadicea*, the Rosyth Shipbreaking Company's last and most significant purchase. It was soon afterwards taken over by the Alloa Shipbreaking Company Ltd.

The Alloa company was soon busy scrapping HMS *Ajax*, which arrived at Rosyth in January 1927, and HMS *King George*, which followed her to

Fig. 54

Top. *Roads within Rosyth Royal Naval Dockyard were named after famous British sea victories and this view shows Camperdown Road.*

Fig. 55

Bottom. *Mess Orderly at Rosyth, still raised the flag each morning in front of the Admiral's Office at Rosyth Royal Naval Dockyard when it was utilised as a ship breaking yard during the years between the two world wars. Here the nameplates from several of the vessels of the German fleet salvaged from the sea-bed at Scapa Flow and towed south for scrapping on the Forth can be seen proudly displayed.*

the breakers in March. That summer the Alloa Company was so busy that it took on thirty-eight extra workmen at Charlestown. Six months later HMS *Colossus* also arrived at the Rosyth breakers and her destruction provided work for a whole year.

Rosyth received its greatest prize to date in May 1928, with the arrival of the German battle-cruiser *Moltke*. The mighty *Moltke*, after which a whole class of battle cruisers was named, was built by Blohm and Voss in their yard at Hamburg, on the Elbe, and launched in 1910. Her salvage was organised by the firm of Cox and Dank, which had been specially established for this work, and she was raised hull-uppermost from the seabed at Scapa Flow, where she had lain in seventy-eight feet of water. Cox and Dank had to obtain special permission from the Admiralty for her to enter Rosyth in this state. Their lordships insisted that extra insurance be taken out and that the hulk be signed over to Admiralty ownership for the duration of the exceedingly tricky operation.

The first attempt to sail the *Moltke* south from the Orkneys to the Forth in this perilous upturned condition was unsuccessful. However, she left her temporary berth at Lyness at the second attempt on Friday 18 May 1928. Somewhat ironically, she was towed by three of the world's most powerful ocean-going tugs, *Pontos*, *See Falke* and *Simson*, all belonging to the German Towage, Freight and Salvage Company of Hamburg, where the *Moltke* had originally taken to the water eighteen years earlier. As the little convoy sailed into the notoriously rough Pentland Firth, it was hit by bad weather and at times the massive hull of the *Moltke* disappeared below the surface. For a time the weight of the *Moltke* began pulling the three tugs in the opposite direction to that in which they were steaming at full speed, but their captains agreed that it was impossible to turn around. Fortunately the winds eased and the tide turned, and the tugs succeeded in regaining control of the huge vessel which had been listing up to twelve degrees. Rounding Duncansby Head, the long slow tow then continued south and the *Moltke* entered the Firth of Forth without further incident.

Then, according to S.C. George in his book *Jutland to Junkyard*, an unexpected drama occurred as she proceeded up the Firth past Leith. He writes:

> Arrangements had been made for an Admiralty pilot to meet the tugs at Inchkeith. However, a Firth of Forth pilot was first on board and when E.F.G. Cox, the director of Cox and Dank, and the engineer who had masterminded the Moltke's salvage arrived with the Admiralty pilot, he refused to give way. Still arguing, the two pilots

Fig. 56

Top. *Labourers at Rosyth
were delighted at the work
provided by the breaking
up of the salvaged vessels
of the German fleet. It
kept them busy during the
inter war years.*

Fig. 57

Bottom. *Naval ratings
busy loading wagons in
Camperdown Road,
named after Admiral
Duncan's famous victory
over the Dutch off the
coast of the Netherlands
in 1797.*

failed to notice that the Forth Bridge was looming up and that the
tide, which had a five-knot run, had carried the tugs to one side of its
central pier while *Moltke* was on the other. The tow rope caught on
Inchgarvie Island in the middle of the Forth, dragging gear off the
stern of one of the tugs. One tug scraped the outlying rock but
fortunately no damage was done. Hastily the cable was cut off. Cox
scarcely dared look, because if the centre bridge was struck by that
tremendous weight, the cost of the resultant damage could ruin him.
But upside-down, engineless and out of control, *Moltke* passed safely
through the central bay and tugs, one lashed either side and one
pulling, took her in tow again and delivered her at Rosyth.

There Number Three Dry Dock had been leased from the Admiralty for her
demolition. Manoeuvring such a large vessel as the *Moltke* into her last
resting place at Rosyth was a very difficult operation. At the highest of
spring-tides the entrance lock had a draught of forty feet. Even with her
superstructure already blasted away, the *Moltke* drew thirty-nine feet, leaving
only inches to spare. As the salvage company knew from past experience that
even the slightest damage to the stone sill of the entrance lock gates involved
them in paying costly repair bills to the Admiralty, a primitive alarm system,
consisting of piano wire stretched across the width of the lock, had been
improvised. This went off as the *Moltke* slowly passed upside-down through
the lock, but, much to E.F.G. Cox's relief, it was discovered to have been
triggered not by the enormous hull of the former German battleship scraping
the bottom, but by a dockyard labourer tapping his foot in time to a popular
tune of the time, which he was whistling.

Another less amusing story connected with the scrapping of the *Moltke*
was that the Scottish labourers working on her demolition were shocked to
discover a heavy, wooden-handled, leather-thonged cat o' nine tails. Was this
simply a rather grisly memento of a bygone age, or had this formidable whip
been used to inflict floggings on the German sailors in her crew as recently as
1918, they were left to wonder.

With the *Moltke* safely delivered to Rosyth work began in Scapa Flow on
the raising of the 24,500-ton German battleship *Kaiser*, whose name had
been given to a whole class of vessels built in 1912 and 1913. Launched at
Kiel on the Baltic in 1911, her final voyage to the Forth was made in ideal
weather conditions.

It was then time to raise the largest of the German naval vessels to be
salvaged so far, the huge battle-cruiser *Hindenburg*. Built at Willhelmshaven
as recently as 1915, her hull now provided the largest amount of scrap metal

Fig. 58

Opposite. *Admiral
Superintendent Rear
Admiral Bovell, Royal
Naval Dockyard Rosyth.*

of any single vessel raised at Scapa Flow. Towed to the Forth by three tugs, she enjoyed an uneventful voyage, and was safely delivered in August 1930 to Metal Industries Ltd, who had taken over the Alloa Shipbreaking Company in November the previous year.

The *Hindenburg* was followed to Rosyth by the battle-cruiser *Seydlitz*, which had been constructed by Blohm and Voss at Hamburg and launched in 1912. Now she suffered an even more storm-tossed passage south from Scapa Flow to the Forth than the *Moltke* had experienced. More difficult still was the tow of the battleship *Prinzregent Luitpold*, built by the shipyard of Germaniawerft in Kiel Bay and launched in 1912. Her voyage from the Orkneys to the breakers in the Forth was delayed by both heavy seas and dense fog, but she finally arrived at Rosyth on 11 May 1932.

Metal Industries, as well as breaking up the vessels of the former German fleet when they finally arrived at Rosyth, also at this point took over from Cox and Dank the task of raising them from the seabed at Scapa Flow.

The complicated work of raising these enormous wrecks continued on into the 1930s and in 1935 the German battleship *Bayern* arrived at the Fife port. Built at Kiel by the yard of Howaldstwerke and launched when the First World War was already underway in 1915, her arrival at Rosyth still attracted much interest. She was opened to the public with tours costing one shilling per person; all of the money collected was given to charities. The *Bayern* yielded rather more in scrap value, her approximately 21,000 tons of steel selling for just over £112,000, providing Metal Industries with a handsome £30,000 profit. That same year the company also broke up the much-loved Cunard liner *Mauretania*, and she too was opened to visitors before the breakers' hammers began to take their toll.

Bayern was followed to Rosyth by the battleship *Konig Albert*, which had been launched at Danzig in 1912. Next came the battleship *Kaiserin*, which had been built at Kiel and launched in 1909, the battleship *Friedrick der Grosse*, built by A.J. Vulcan of Hamburg and launched in 1911, and the battleship *Grosser Kurfurst*, also built by A.J. Vulcan, but not launched until 1915. Together these five massive vessels provided just under 100,000 tons of scrap. Ironically, large quantities of this armoured steel plating was exported to Germany for the construction of Hitler's mighty new naval fleet. However, it was only when the new German government attempted to purchase heavy artillery from the scrapped battleships that the Admiralty was notified. Not only were export licenses refused, but word was sent to Rosyth ordering that all of the guns were to be destroyed immediately.

Amidst these growing fears that Germany might again consider waging war, the Admiralty in 1936 decided to train more naval ratings at Rosyth.

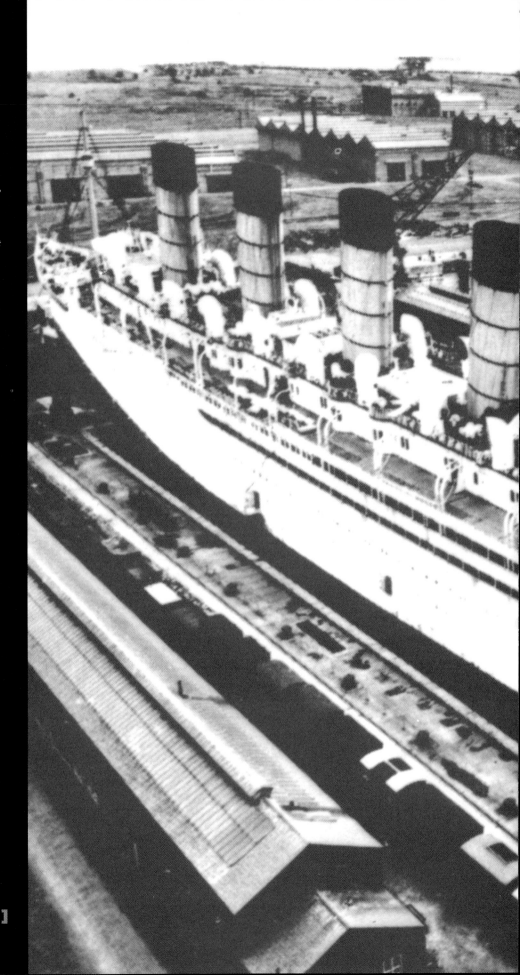

Fig. 59
Mauretania *in Rosyth
Docks for breaking up.*

Mauretania *was built by
Swan Hunter and
Wigham Richardson Ltd,
Newcastle and launched
on the Tyne in 1907.
31,938 tons and 790 feet
long, she carried 2,335
passengers at a service
speed of 25 knots. She
held the transatlantic
speed record for longer
than any other vessel.*

MAURETANIA AT ROSYTH

Fig. 60

HMS Caledonia *sank off Blackness when a disastrous fire gutted her during the early days of the Second World War. Her burnt-out hull was eventually salvaged in 1943 to provide scrap for the war effort.*

Faced with the problem of where to billet them, the Admiralty came up with idea of purchasing the White Star Line's luxury liner *Majestic*, which had conveniently just arrived in the Forth to be scrapped. Her career had been cut short by the government-enforced merger of her owners with Cunard as a condition of releasing funds for the completion of the *Queen Mary* at John Brown's at Clydebank on the River Clyde.

The *Majestic* was originally built in Germany during the First World War as Hamburg – America Line's *Bismarck*. When she was launched she was the world's largest passenger ocean liner, a claim to fame which she held until the launch of the French-owned *Normandie* in 1935, and her maiden voyage was intended to provide the Kaiser with a triumphant world cruise to celebrate his country's expected victory. Instead, following the Armistice, she was seized by the Allies as part of the reparations which the Germans were forced to make and, as a result, came under the flag of the famous British White Star Line, as her new name, *Majestic*, indicated (all of the company's vessels had names ending in the letters '-ic', including, of course, the ill fated *Titanic*).

The Admiralty regarded it as a particular triumph that it succeeded in acquiring the *Majestic* as its new naval training ship without having to pay out any money. This was achieved by persuading the breakers to accept in exchange twenty-four small redundant naval vessels as equivalent to the value of the *Majestic*, which was set at £115,500.

As soon as she was alongside at Rosyth, *Majestic* was renamed HMS *Caledonia*, and work began on equipping her as a floating boarding-school for 2,000 young naval recruits. Her engines had been stripped out before her

Fig. 61

While the censor deleted part of the picture of the hull of the former training ship HMS Caledonia, *the story of how it was raised from the bed of the Forth was released to the press, as the amount of scrap obtained was in 1943 considered a suitably morale-boosting news item. She was originally built in Germany as the world's largest passenger liner* Bismarck *(although she never sailed under that name, being acquired by Britain as war reparations after the First World War).*

Fig. 62

*The tangled hull of the
former training-vessel
HMS* Caledonia *after it
was raised from the bed of
the Forth in 1943.*

voyage under tow from Liverpool to the Forth and even this cavernous space
was used to fit in more dormitories for the boy trainees. The career of HMS
Caledonia as a training establishment came to an abrupt halt on Sunday 3
September 1939, when the declaration of war raised fears at the Admiralty
that the Germans might well seek revenge for the seizure back in 1918 of
their proud new liner and, out of spite, make her one of the first targets of
the new hostilities. This threat was taken particularly seriously because
British Intelligence had reported that the Air Attaché to the German Embassy
in London, Captain Spiller, had himself flown low over the ship only days
before. Accompanied by his wife, he had taken off from the recently
constructed aerodrome at nearby Grangemouth on the south side of the
Forth and flown down the river at the start of one of the legs of his Scottish
tour, which was officially logged as a 'holiday journey'.

With these fears in mind, the 2,000 boy sailors plus their instructors and
officers were all ordered hurriedly to disembark from the ship. Even empty,
HMS *Caledonia* was considered a hazard to the safety of Rosyth. If she were
to be hit and damaged during a German air-raid, her engine-less hull might
prove difficult to remove. She was therefore towed out of the naval dockyard
upriver, where she was deliberately beached on a mud-bank off Blackness.
Only three weeks later, on 29 September, a fire broke out on board. The
blaze spread rapidly throughout the entire vessel, lighting up the night sky as
crowds lined both sides of the Forth to watch the spectacle. The burnt-out
hulk lay in the Forth for two years until it was eventually towed to Ward's
shipbreaking yard at Inverkeithing. The mighty size of the hull can be judged

from the fact that it took the breakers two years to dispose finally of this remarkable vessel, which in the days of her transatlantic glory had been given the affectionate nickname of the 'Lucky Stick' by her White Star Line crew.

Back in 1936, at the same time the *Majestic* arrived on the scene at Rosyth, a campaign began to put the Royal Naval Dockyard back on a working footing. Its supporters were encouraged when in October the Home Fleet visited the Forth for the first time for two years. While they were in the river, several of the vessels were opened to the public.

One year later, in the autumn of 1937, the First Sea Lord, Duff Cooper, sailed in aboard the Admiralty yacht *Enchantress*. With her graceful lines, this beautiful vessel drew much attention as she lay at anchor just upriver from the Forth Bridge.

Meanwhile, shipbreaking continued to be the main business at Rosyth; Metal Industries was kept busy throughout 1938 with the scrapping of the passenger liner *Leviathan*, plus a series of American cargo vessels which the Scottish company had bought as a job lot.

In the background, however, the government was preparing for the possibility of the start of hostilities. A boom defence was constructed off Cramond Island, and then, in December 1938, it was announced that the naval dockyard was to reopen on a limited scale. Metal Industries was informed by the Admiralty that its lease of Dry Dock Number Three for shipbreaking purposes was to be terminated, as it was required for other more urgent business, including the refit of aircraft carriers. The hulk of the German battle-cruiser *Derfflinger*, which was to have been brought south for scrapping, was retained at Scapa Flow. She remained there for the duration of the war and, after it was over, was sent to Faslane on the Gare Loch on the River Clyde.

In early 1939 the workforce at Rosyth was rapidly increased from 573 to over 1,000 and by September the dockyard employed 1,670 men. HMS *Cochrane* arrived to replace HMS *Greenwich* as the base's depot ship, and in June two cruisers belonging to the French navy, the *Georges Leygues* and the *Montcalm*, joined the ships of the British Home Fleet on a visit.

As that long hot summer drew to a close, Britain warned Germany that unless she withdrew from Poland, Britain would commence hostilities. The ultimatum was ignored by Hitler and his government, and at 11 a.m. on Sunday 3 September the Forth again became a river at war.

Rosyth received the first casualty of the Second World War when, on Monday 25 September, the damaged submarine HMS *Spearfish* was towed into the Naval Dockyard to undergo repairs.

Fig. 63

The 9082-ton British India Steam Navigation Company Ltd troopship Neuralia *visited Leith on several occasions during the 1930s, to embark not soldiers but schoolboys. This was the start of the pioneering school-cruises which the line operated during summer holiday periods, when there was a lull in trooping contracts because of the severe heat in the Mediterranean and the Suez Canal. In this picture-postcard view, taken to sell to the pupils aboard,* Neuralia *is seen passing through the Kiel Canal between the River Elbe and the Baltic. These school-cruises were brought to an abrupt halt by the approach of war in 1939. Edinburgh pupils booked to travel on* Neuralia's *summer holiday cruise in 1939 were disappointed when it was cancelled only weeks before they were scheduled to embark. Like all ships belonging to British India,* Neuralia *had a name ending in the letter 'a', and when, in 1961, the company reintroduced the idea of school-cruises,* Dunera, Devonia, Nevasa *and* Uganda *became famous.*

[3]

THE SECOND WORLD WAR

AIR RAID ON THE FORTH

Excitement was even greater three weeks later when, on 15 October, the strategic importance of the Forth was recognised by the Germans, when they made it the scene of their first attack on mainland Britain. Early that morning, enemy reconnaissance aircraft were spotted high above the river, but they disappeared before they could be challenged. Shortly after two in the afternoon, however, the air-raid sirens wailed again. This time, an entire formation of twelve German bombers was reported to be flying in formation from the North Sea inland along the course of the Forth Estuary towards the Forth Bridge, below which lay several navy vessels.

The Spitfires of the City of Edinburgh Squadron 603 of the RAF were immediately scrambled at Turnhouse Airport and, within minutes, took off to intercept the approaching enemy. First contact was logged at 2.35 p.m., when the Spitfires spotted two enemy aircraft flying off the May Island at the mouth of the Firth. From then on, the Spitfires harried the German Dornier DO 17s and Heinkel HE 111s as they flew on with their distinctive drone past Dunbar and North Berwick. Soon dogfights began and two of the bombers were brought down. One was chased north across the Forth and crashed near Crail on the Fife shore. The second ditched into the river off the fishing harbour of Port Seton. Its crew parachuted out before it hit the water and they were fortunate to be picked up by the Port Seton-registered fishing boat, *Dayspring*. To show his gratitude at being rescued, the German pilot took off his gold signet ring and presented it to the skipper of the *Dayspring*. It is still in the possession of his family.

Meanwhile, the other ten German bombers flew on up the Firth past Musselburgh, Portobello, Leith and Cramond, and succeeded in reaching the Forth Bridge. Down below it in the little town of Queensferry, despite the air-raid siren having sounded, many of the local folk still thought that it was only a practice and stood staring skyward at the fast-approaching enemy planes and the RAF Spitfires which were firing at them. To add to the

Queensferry (Firth of Forth)
Hilfsstützpunkt Port Edgar

westl. Greenw. 3 23 20 Breite 56 0 0
Mißweisung -13°24 Mitte 1939 Zielhöhe über N.N. 50m

Nachtrage
2. 10. 39.

500 0 500 1000
m
Maßstab etwa 1 : 15 000   150 m

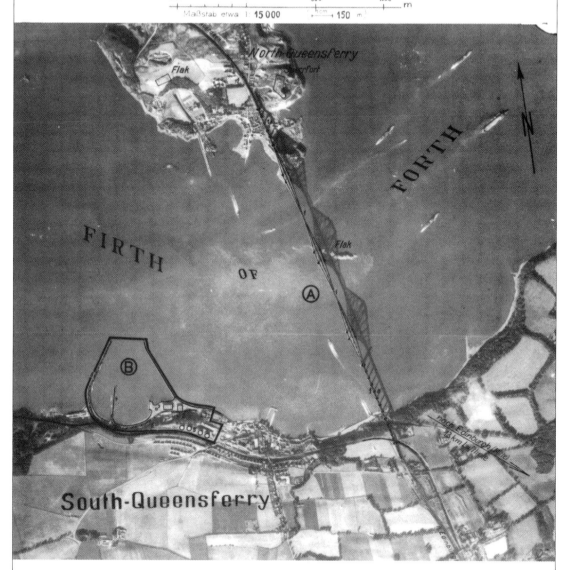

Ⓑ   GB *12 12*   South Queensferry - Port Edgar
(Hilfsstützpunkt)

Ⓐ   GB 41 6 Eisenbahnbrücke über den Firth of Forth

1) 2 Stahlbrückenbogen auf 3 Hauptpfeilern, in je
   massiven Fundamentblocken verankert
1a) 2 Viadukte mit 17 Steinpfeilern
   Bruckengesamtlänge etwa 2500 m, Breite etwa 8m

2) 5 Depothallen   etwa 6 300 qm
3) 2 Tanks: 1 große Ø etwa 15m, 2 kleire Ø ca 5m
                                                etwa 4 200 qm
4) Lager mit Gleisanschluß
5) Kai mit Kranbahnkran
6) Verwaltungsgebäude
   Gebäude zu etwa etwa 13 200 qm

Fig. 65

The spans of the Forth Railway Bridge, with Inchgarvie below it, can be seen from this naval vessel at her base in Rosyth during the Second World War.

confusion, as the planes loomed overhead, the town's air-raid siren sounded the all-clear signal. Up on the level of the bridge's southern end, at Dalmeny Railway Station, the station master had halted a passenger train which was about to steam out over the river, thanks to the original air-raid warning. As he and the porters raced along the length of the carriages which made up the train, trying to persuade the passengers that this was not a practice drill but an actual attack, the engine-driver distinctly heard the all-clear signal being sounded by the siren down on the roof of the police station in Queensferry High Street. He in turn sounded his horn and drove the train out of the station and onto the bridge, where it reached the central span just as the leading three German bombers dived overhead.

Fortunately for the passengers and the crew of the train, the German pilots appear to have honoured the code then still recognised – that they should not bomb civilian targets. And so instead of launching their bombs on the bridge, they concentrated their attack on the ships of the British fleet at anchor in the river below. The three Royal Naval vessels involved were the two cruisers HMS *Edinburgh* and HMS *Southampton* and the destroyer HMS *Mohawk*. As the volley of German bombs rained down, the *Southampton* suffered a direct hit, making her the first British naval surface

Fig. 66

Sailors stood to attention as sunset was piped aboard this naval vessel in the Forth.

vessel to be damaged in the Second World War. The same bomb also sank the admiral's barge, which happened to be alongside *Southampton* at the time, and an accompanying small naval steam pinnace. Three of her ship's company were injured by flying shrapnel. HMS *Edinburgh* and HMS *Mohawk* escaped undamaged, but three of the crew of the former and twenty-five of the crew of the latter were injured during the attack, bringing the total British casualties during the raid to thirty-one.

As the train reached the Fife side of the bridge at North Queensferry, its passengers, who had had a grandstand view of all of the action, watched as a third bomber was brought down by the guns of the anti-aircraft battery on the shore below. A few moments later, another of the Spitfires scored a direct hit on a fourth German bomber, which was trying to escape by flying south, and it was brought down over the Pentland Hills.

Although the Forth Bridge had not been attacked directly in this surprise raid, the attack alerted the British military authorities as to how important a target it might prove in the future. Its destruction would play havoc with communications with the north of Scotland, and also provide the Germans with a great propaganda coup, as it was such a well-known structure world-wide. It was therefore decided at the highest level that its vulnerability must

Fig. 67
*The first German aircraft
to fall on British soil was
this Heinkel He III, which
crash-landed on a hillside
near Haddington on 28
October 1939.The
photograph shows RAF
personnel, and a local
schoolboy, inspecting the
wreckage the following
day.*

Fig. 68
*In October 1939 the
Luftwaffe scored a direct
hit on the British cruiser
HMS Edinburgh. This
photograph, taken by a
German pilot, shows the
resulting explosion behind
the second funnel on the
ship's port side.*

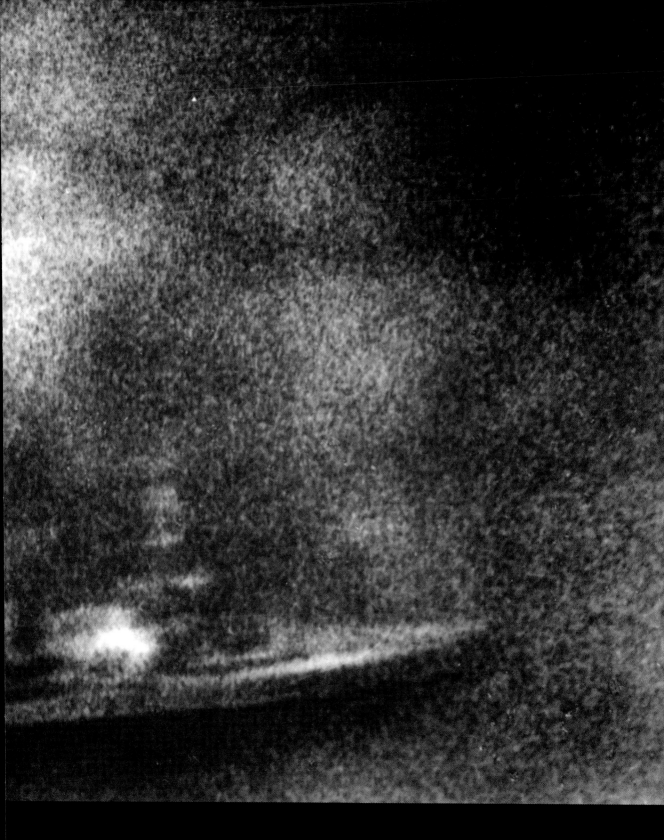

Fig. 70

Drem Aerodrome, near North Berwick in East Lothian, was a hive of activity when this photograph was taken in 1943. Hispano shells are seen being loaded aboard a Beau Fighter.

be reduced, and this was done by creating a special barrage battalion. Nearby Dundas Castle was requisitioned as its headquarters, and, within weeks, the Forth Bridge was protected by the huge grey whale-like barrage balloons which loomed over it for the remainder of the war. Local people claim they knew the likelihood of an attack from the height at which the barrage balloons were positioned. When they flew high, they could relax, but when the balloons huddled low over the maroon-painted cantilever spans of the bridge, they realised that their sleep was likely to be disturbed by yet another air raid. The barrage balloons were a very effective defence and, despite several subsequent efforts after they had abandoned the promise not to bomb civilian sites, the Germans never managed to inflict any damage on the Forth Bridge. So desperately did they wish to do so, however, that it is claimed they deliberately took an out-of-focus photograph on one of their raids and later published it upside-down in their newspapers, claiming that the black blur of Inchgarvie Island was the dust and debris of a successful hit scored on the famous bridge.

At this time the strength of the RAF was also increased, with bases on both shores of the Forth, including Crail, near Fife Ness and Drem, in East Lothian, where the commanding officer was Wing Commander A.D.

Farquhar, DFC. At nearby East Fortune, where the Scottish National Air Museum is now housed, a large sanatorium for tuberculosis patients was evacuated inland to Bangour near Bathgate, West Lothian, to allow for the expansion of the RAF fighter base.

HOW THE SECOND WORLD WAR
AFFECTED CIVILIANS IN CITY AND COUNTRYSIDE

The German air attack on the Forth in October 1939 did not take the people of Edinburgh, the Lothians and Fife entirely by surprise. They well remembered the night during the First World War when a German Zeppelin launched an attack on the capital, an event portrayed in one of the stained glass windows in the Scottish National War Museum subsequently opened at Edinburgh Castle. The great fear in the run up to the announcement of hostilities again in 1939 was that gas would be used on the civilian population. As a precaution, gas masks were issued. Protection against attack was even available for babies in the form of a gas mask shaped like a cradle while, for children, an attempt was made to make their black gas masks look less menacing by manufacturing them with Mickey Mouse ears.

For children the announcement of Britain's entry into the war over the wireless on Sunday 3 September brought an unexpected bonus in the extension of the summer holidays. It was decided that schools should not re-open as scheduled the following Tuesday, as it was feared that German air raids might inflict many casualties in the classrooms since shelters had still to be constructed in school playgrounds.

According to the entry to the log for one Lothian school for 5 September, 'Intimation has been received that classes will not resume until provision has been made for the children in the event of an air attack.' Two weeks later, however, the youngsters' fun was somewhat spoilt. Although the entry for 19 September begins, 'School still closed,' it continues, 'Teachers met to consider what might be done to occupy the children's time during the day and effect some control over their activities.' The general plan was for each teacher to issue assignments of work to be done at home. For this purpose each class was divided into groups of five with a leader. 'The duty of the leader is to distribute the homework to the members of the group and to collect and return to the teacher the written exercises. Where such is possible the teacher on returning the corrected work sends a message to those needing attention drawn to errors to visit her at her home. There is no doubt about the faithfulness of the teachers' service and of the response of many of the pupils, but

Fig. 71

Sailors with fixed bayonets march along Princes Street in Edinburgh. Events such as this were frequently staged as part of Navy Weeks to persuade the civilian population to raise funds for the war effort. The salute is being taken from the steps of the Royal Scottish Academy at the foot of the Mound.

The Nelson Monument, is the shape of the admiral's upturned telescope, is seen on the top of Calton Hill. To the left is what is often known as 'Scotland's Folly', the war memorial designed to commemorate those killed in the Napoleonic Wars, which was never finished because of lack of funds.

Fig. 72

Top. *Huge crowds turned out to line Princes Street for events during Navy Week. Edinburgh policemen still wore helmets during the war years, as this photograph taken on the pavement outside the popular Fifty Shilling Tailors shows. Notice the schoolboy on the right carrying his gas mask in its cardboard container on a strap over his shoulder.*

Fig. 73

Bottom. *This inspection of naval ratings took place on the same day on the cobbled forecourt of the National Gallery of Scotland at the foot of the Mound.*

Fig. 74

Top. *On a wartime Sunday morning this column of members of the ATS marched down the esplanade of Edinburgh Castle to take part in church parade.*

Fig. 75

Bottom. *Crowds lined the Mound as they marched down it and onto Princes Street.*

Fig. 76

Left. *The salute was taken on the steps of the Royal Scottish Academy, with officers of the ATS also on parade, wearing the tartan kilts which were part of the uniform.*

Fig. 77

Right. *After the church parade concluded there was an opportunity for the officers to chat.*

the voluntary nature of the work has afforded for some a sufficient excuse for the minimum of effort! The teachers of the infant department have gone on peripatetic duty. Several mothers have very generously given a room in their homes for small groups to meet and good work is being done.'

These schooling arrangements continued during October, when many teachers were also deployed in the writing of and issue of ration books. From then on coupons were required to ensure the fair distribution of a growing number of foodstuffs and household supplies.

Pupils did not finally return to many schools until the first week in November, by which time brick-built shelters with reinforced concrete roofs had hurriedly been erected adjacent to most schools. Air raid drills were introduced, with warnings issued to the boys and girls that any misbehaviour while sitting in the crowded blacked-out shelters would be severely dealt with by the infliction of strokes of the leather tawse, and that forgetting to carry gas masks in their regulation brown cardboard boxes would also be deemed a strapable offence.

Even more worrying for the children was the threat that they might soon be forced to leave their homes under emergency evacuation plans then being drawn up. An Edinburgh school logbook entry of the time reads, 'Teachers stayed late to complete a survey of those children whose parents wish them to leave the city and of the accommodation to be utilised in the event of

Figs. 78 & 79
Soldiers were given a hero's welcome when they disembarked at Leith docks during the war.

Figs. 80 & 81

WVS volunteers were on hand to offer welcome cups of tea to the soldiers who disembarked at Leith Docks.

evacuation being put into effect.'

Out of a total of 33,150 Edinburgh families with school-age children who were surveyed, only 12,642 indicated that they wished their children to participate in the evacuation scheme. In the event, 26,000 children were evacuated, just over 40 per cent of those eligible. Those who were pupils at inner city schools were ordered to assemble in their playgrounds, complete with obligatory luggage labels attached to their coats giving their names, addresses and dates of birth. Amongst tearful scenes they were then marched to Waverley and Haymarket Stations, where fleets of carriages formed long trains pulled by steam locomotives to take them to unknown destinations in other parts of Scotland. Some of the Edinburgh children were billeted on families living as close by as Linlithgow and Galashiels, while others were transported as far away as Inverness. Mix-ups were common and the actual children who arrived at the various destinations often did not match with the lists of names of those expected, and hastily recruited billeting officers, who were often members of the local Women's Voluntary Service or Red Cross, struggled to try to keep brothers and sisters together while matching them

with the accommodation available.

Many of the Edinburgh children came from the poorer, overcrowded parts of the city and there was often a considerable culture clash between them and the people of the communities they were evacuated to. In Linlithgow, for instance, several boys were landed on the town's largest mansion, the hilltop House of Grange. Its owner, the late Mrs Cadell, later recalled that

> One day a billeting officer arrived and decided that my home was big enough to take no fewer than eight evacuees. I was given a choice, not whether or not I wanted the evacuees, but whether to accept boys or girls. I chose boys and they duly arrived from Edinburgh. We did have room for them in the nursery, but we simply didn't have eight beds, so as County Commissioner for West Lothian for the Girl Guides, I burgled the guide hut in the grounds of the house and found eight palliasses. These I took to the farmer at Erngath and persuaded him to fill them with straw, so the little boys had

Fig. 82

Top. *There was considerable concern in Edinburgh, as in other parts of Great Britain, that the enemy would launch a poison gas attack on the country. Here Edinburgh-based ATS recruits are seen being inspected by one of their officers as they don gas masks.*

Fig. 83

Bottom. *A careful watch was kept on the health of Edinburgh's children throughout the war years and, ironically, the effects of rationing and more regular inspections by school nurses helped to improve conditions. At school each child received a third of a pint of milk each morning before playtime, and mothers were issued with supplies of cod liver oil and unsweetened concentrated orange juice. The children may not have appreciated the taste, but these things were much better for them than their pre-war diet of jelly pieces, sugar-laden tea, sweets and chocolate, all of which were now in short supply because of rationing.*

Fig. 84
Because of the demand for materials for the war-effort, toys were also in very short supply, but children's wartime Christmases were often brightened by the gift of home-made soft toys, such as this (now very un-politically-correct) golliwog, proudly displayed by an ATS officer.

something to lie on for the night. Next day they started school at West Port. The townsfolk of Linlithgow were really very kind to them. At lunchtime the lady in the grocer's shop on the corner of High Street and St Ninian's Road gave them cups of hot soup in those days before the first school meals were introduced in 1942, but they missed the city and were not very happy. As the phoney war dragged on and nothing very much in the way of air raids occurred in Edinburgh, several of the mothers came out to take their sons home. The boys were having a meal in the day nursery when they arrived and when one of the mothers heard I was being paid five shillings a week to look after her boys, she declared that she thought that I was being paid a fortune! The remainder of the evacuees left soon after as my own children caught scarlet fever.

Mrs Cadell makes no mention of her family also catching head lice, scabies and impetigo, but all of these conditions affected many Forth country families who took city evacuee children into their homes, and many were shocked at the lack of cleanliness amongst their uninvited young guests. One

Fig. 85

Rosyth is seen from the air in this reconnaissance photograph taken by an enemy German plane flying on a spy mission high above the Royal Naval Dockyard. Notice how carefully it was annotated. The three dry docks are clearly visible.

Forth Valley local newspaper reported that a councillor described the evacuation scheme as the biggest shock which his constituents had received since the Industrial Revolution. 'It has lifted the veil on the lives of thousands of the populace,' he complained, 'disclosing such conditions of squalor, disease, dirt and ignorance of the elementary laws of health and decent living that it has appalled those of us who have had to cope. We had to start delousing both persons and bedding!'

As well as billeting city evacuees on individual households in surrounding country towns, larger numbers of children were also accommodated in two specially constructed school camps at Broomlee, near the village of West Linton in Peeblesshire and in the grounds of Middleton Hall, near Gorebridge in Midlothian, as well as in several large mansions which were requisitioned for the purpose, including Clarendon House in Linlithgow and Luffness House, near Aberlady in East Lothian.

The choice of East Lothian as a safe refuge for many Edinburgh children is in hindsight a puzzling one. There was a great deal of war-related activity in the county as the authorities considered early in the hostilities that if

-978 NLA14 IPRU 19·6·41 1/20 S↓

Fig. 86
*Rosyth docks from the air.
On the windward
perimeter of the port anti-
aircraft landing ditches
were dug in case of
invasion, while anti-
aircraft positions were
installed to attempt to
ward off attacks from
the air.*

Edinburgh were ever invaded the enemy would land to the east on the south
shore of the Firth of Forth. The whole sweep of coastline from Leith to St
Abbs Head was therefore declared a restricted area and checkpoints were set
up and manned twenty-four hours a day on all roads leading into the area.
These conditions were also imposed on the coast from Newhaven west
upriver to Grangemouth. All vehicles entering these areas were stopped and
searched, while the identity cards of drivers and passengers were carefully
checked, and only those with residence certificates or special permission
documents were allowed to enter any of the towns and villages which had
docks or harbours. Similar restrictions were also imposed all along the coast
of Fife.

How seriously the threat of invasion was taken can be judged from the
remains of the concrete gun emplacements, pill boxes and concrete tank traps
which can still be seen along the shores of the Forth, despite the major clean
up operation of 1963 aimed at removing many of them. A minefield was
deliberately laid by the Allies along the south shore of the Forth, while on the
neighbouring shore coastal defence anti-aircraft batteries and searchlight

Fig. 87

Top. *As Musselburgh is situated on the coast of the Firth of Forth, this gun was positioned to guard the bridge carrying the main road over the River Esk, which it was thought would be a vulnerable target in the event of a German invasion from the sea. Concrete road blocks were positioned at the bridge in June 1940, resulting in the tram service along Musselburgh High Street being reduced to single track operations. This caused major inconvenience to local residents, and as the worry over imminent invasion declined, the obstructions were removed at the end of July, allowing Edinburgh Corporation Transport to resume normal service.*

Fig. 88

Bottom. *Defence precautions were taken along the length of Princes Street. This pill-box, incongruously camouflaged as a florist's shop, was erected on the broad pavement outside the Rutland Hotel at the West End.*

Fig. 89

Top. *A similar, but this time uncamouflaged, pill-box was erected on the opposite side of Lothian Road outside St John's Scottish Episcopal Church. Tram-tracks ran down the middle of Lothian Road and on along Princes Street. The overhead electric cables which supplied the trams with power are clearly visible. Throughout the war, the blackout was strictly enforced on the trams. Their headlights were painted black, apart from narrow slits to let a small shaft of light shine through, and the blinds were pulled down over the windows, both on the lower and upper decks as soon as dusk fell.*

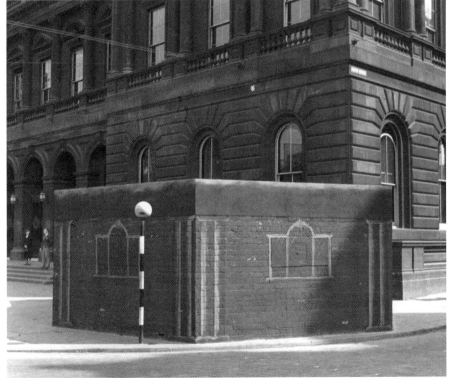

Fig. 90

Bottom. *At the opposite end of Princes Street there was another strangely camouflaged pill-box on the corner of Waterloo Place outside the General Post Office, which is visible in the background. During the war years post office customers were encouraged to save paper by using sticky labels to reseal envelopes.*

Fig. 91

Street signs were taken down, not just to deny the enemy information in the event of an invasion, but, as in this case, to help the war effort by stockpiling metal. Garden railings throughout the city were removed and stockpiled at Leith Docks with this same aim in mind, but after the war it was admitted that the wrought iron which they yielded was totally unsuitable and that this exercise had been mainly intended to keep up the morale of the civilian population by convincing them that such a sacrifice was helping the war effort.

Fig. 92

Top. *The sloop HMS
Barry at Port Edgar, with
the Forth Railway Bridge
in the background.*

Fig. 93

Middle. *Sailors at work on
the barrel of an eight-inch
pom-pom gun.*

Fig. 94

Bottom. *A boom defence
was also laid to give added
protection from submarine
attack and mine laying
activity to vessels in the
Forth.*

Fig. 95

Opposite. *This warship,
photographed in the Firth
of Forth, bristled with
guns.*

Fig. 96
A group of destroyers
leaves harbour ahead
of the fleet.

Fig. 97

Top. *Many Edinburgh women were employed on war work, including making camouflage nets.*

Fig. 98

Opposite. *Each day wireless programmes were transmitted on the National Programme of the BBC, and shows such as 'Music While You Work' at 10.30 a.m. and 'Workers' Playtime' at 12.30 p.m. were eagerly awaited. For workers such as this woman putting leaves on a camouflage net, the programmes helped break the monotony of such tasks. 'Workers' Playtime', which was on several occasions transmitted live from the canteens of factories around Edinburgh, was first broadcast in 1941 and was so popular that it continued for many years after the war, until finally taken off the air in 1963.*

Fig. 99

Right. *Other Scottish women enjoyed a more exciting war as motor cycle messengers; some are pictured here while on an exercise in a wood on the outskirts of the city.*

Fig. 100

*The war provided many
new opportunities for
Scottish women, including
working as motor
mechanics, as seen in this
photograph, which the
censor merely describes as
'taken near Edinburgh'.*

Fig. 101

*Opposite. Edinburgh's
'Dad's Army' even took to
the water in a combined
exercise with the Royal
Navy on the Water of
Leith, as seen here in a
photograph taken in front
of the Caledonia Mills. A
touch of realism was
added to this water-based
exercise by equipping the
motor launch with a
Lewis gun.*

positions to illuminate enemy targets by night stretched all the way from
Direlton, near North Berwick, to Merrilees, overlooking Blackness Castle,
well upriver to the west.

The use of powerful searchlights, which could be triggered immediately
when radio observation stations at Haddington, North Berwick and Belhaven
House (now home of Belhaven Preparatory School, near Dunbar, but
previously where Special Operation Agents were trained for missions behind
enemy lines) picked up the sound of enemy aircraft, contrasted with the total
blackout imposed on both city and country. Department stores such as Binns,
which occupied the corner site at the west end of Princes Street, advertised
special sales of blackout materiel. The blackout was strictly imposed by the
officers of the ARP (the Air Raid Prevention service), who, after their normal
day's work had regularly to stay up throughout the night manning rooftop
positions on tall buildings, ranging from Jenners department store in Princes
Street to the Shrubhill depot of Edinburgh Corporation Transport
Department.

The Second World War placed a great burden on public transport in

Edinburgh (at a time when petrol rationing limited fuel for private motoring to thirty miles a month), as it had to cope with a great increase in passengers during a period when everything from staff to spare parts became in increasingly short supply. While tram cars and buses continued to operate after dark (despite having their headlights blacked out to leave only narrow slits to emit the minimum of light), the blackout totally prevented any of the maintenance work which was usually carried out on the tracks during the night hours. Shortage of fuel even for vitally needed public transport led to the curtailment of evening services and of routes, and nine single-decker buses were converted to be powered by gas, which was stored in enormous bags towed behind on two-wheeled trailers.

As more and more men were enlisted into the armed services, the problem of staff shortage was tackled by the introduction, for the first time, of women, who were employed as conductresses from May 1941. At first they were confined to duties on single-decker buses so that passengers did not receive so much as a glimpse of stocking as they climbed the stairs, but soon wartime demands scuppered such sensitivities and women were allocated to work on double-decker buses and trams. Bright red painted honesty boxes were also introduced on the entrance platforms of buses and trams in the hope that passengers would deposit unpaid fares on crowded rush hour services. One route on which vehicles were always packed was the one introduced in September 1942 to help transport the increased wartime workforce to and from the engineering works at Crewe Toll.

Another major Edinburgh employer that saw a huge increase in its workforce – to a total of around 2000 – was the Brunton wireworks at Musselburgh. This company manufactured a number of products for the war effort, including pre-stressed catapult hawsers used in the launching of planes from aircraft carriers. The Brunton factory was one of many in the city where workers operated round the clock on three eight-hour shifts, but it still managed to support its own branch of the Home Guard. Many other city factories, including shipbuilders Henry Robb and Menzies at Leith, also encouraged their men to join the new Home Guard, and to save time and transport provided facilities on their premises for the men to meet and drill.

Founded originally on 14 May 1940 as the Local Defence Volunteers by Secretary of State for War Anthony Eden, the organisation was officially re-named the Home Guard only two months later by wartime leader Winston Churchill. One of the Edinburgh battalions of the Home Guard had its headquarters at Holyrood Palace and carried out practices in Holyrood Park. Although handicapped by lack of weapons, the members of the Home Guard, who have been immortalised by the popular BBC television series,

Fig. 102
Home Guard exercises often took place in the streets of the Scottish capital; on this occasion one of the city's old red phone boxes appears to have become the object of suspicion. The white bands on the young soldiers' caps indicate that they were officer cadets.

Fig. 103

Top. *An officer cadet leads his men on this exercise in an Edinburgh city street. This may now appear to be playing at soldiers, but at the time, with the ever-present threat of German invasion, these practice drills were taken very seriously.*

Fig. 104

Bottom. *Three members of Edinburgh Home Guard are seen here taking aim through the castellations of a pill-box, from where, in the event of a real invasion, it was expected that they would engage the Germans in street fighting.*

Dad's Army, did much to maintain morale amongst the civilian population in Edinburgh and all of the surrounding towns. Branches drilled every week to provide an immediate local response in the event of the expected invasion by enemy forces.

Meanwhile local householders were kept equally occupied excavating sites in their back gardens in which to conceal the Anderson shelters, which were issued to provide refuge for families in the event of air raids. These corrugated iron prefabricated structures were named after the War Cabinet minister who was responsible for their issue. As well as the basic shell of the shelter, which was sunk into the ground and covered with a protective layer of earth, each kit came with pre-cut lengths of timber to build four bunk beds, as it was feared that families might have to spend many long nights huddled underground. Fortunately, however, although Edinburgh and the surrounding area did suffer occasional attacks form the air, such as the one on Leith on 18 July 1940, when a hit-and-run raider dropped a single bomb, resulting in a large crater at the road junction at Portland Place, and another raid on 9 November 1939, the raid of 3 November 1940 which destroyed the new Co-operative Society store at North Berwick and that of 3 March 1941 on Haddington during which the audience in the New County Cinema had a narrow escape when a nearby garage and shops were damaged, the much feared Blitz which occurred that year in the west of Scotland on Clydebank never happened in the Forth Valley.

Preparing for an invasion which never came was a thankless task, but the members of the Home Guard kept up their spirits with drills and weekend camps, such as the one held in the grounds of Gosford House, near Longniddry, in 1940. Later in the war Gosford became an army base, and after the success of the D-Day landings in June 1944, Gosford's extensive estate was selected to house a large camp for 3,000 German prisoners of war. So many captured Germans were sent to Scotland that an overflow camp was also established at Amisfield near Haddington. There were a few abortive escape attempts, but the vast majority of the defeated Germans accepted their captivity and settled down to await the end of the war, which they realised was drawing to a close. The unexpected availability of all of this manpower was utilised to good effect when POWs were formed into work squads to help on local farms, which were struggling because so many of the local men had been called up.

The German prisoners were not the only strangers who appeared on the scene in the countryside around the shores of the Forth during the Second World War. Members of the Women's Land Army were also recruited to help ease the labour shortage on Lothian farms. Mainly from Scottish towns and

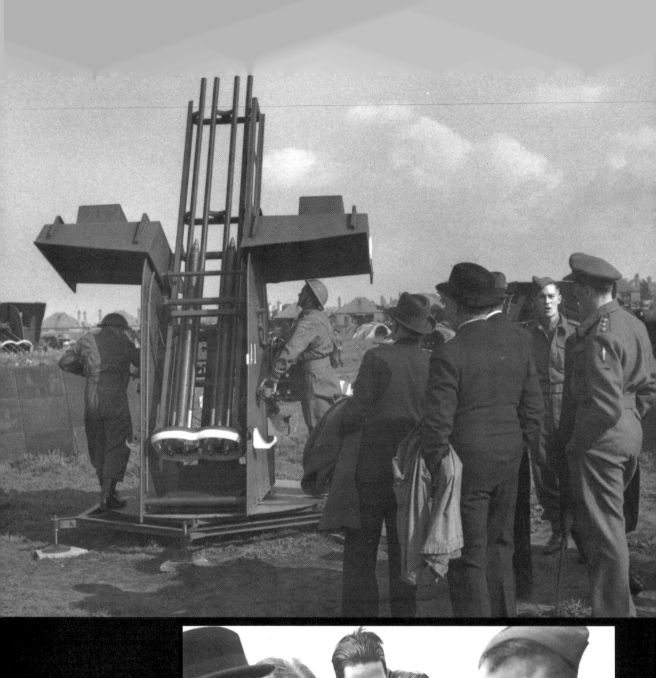

Figs. 105 to 108

To encourage them to report the war efforts in a positive fashion, the editors of Edinburgh-based newspapers, including The Scotsman, The Evening News *and* The Evening Despatch, *were invited to witness this army exercise on the outskirts of the city.*

Figs. 109 to 111

With hindsight, many Home Guard exercises appear to have been futile, such as this search for booby traps in a garden on the outskirts of Edinburgh at Liberton.

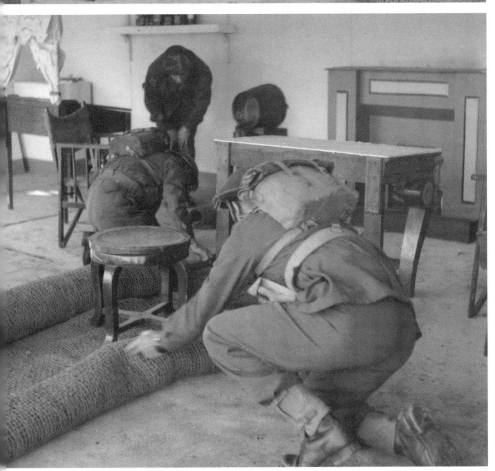

Fig. 112
*Edinburgh did suffer
several air raids, including
one which caused this
damage to George Watson's
Boys' College. This
independent fee-paying
school continued to hold
classes throughout the war,
as did its equivalent school
for girls in George Square.
Children from primary
schools in more crowded
housing-scheme areas of the
city were offered the choice
of being evacuated to
neighbouring towns such as
Bathgate and Linlithgow,
where they were billeted
with local families, or to
camp schools. These latter
included Middleton Camp
School near Gorebridge and
Broomlee Camp School in
the Southern Uplands near
the village of West Linton.
Each camp could
accommodate over 300
pupils plus teachers and the
schools were well equipped
with what were described
as 'sun-trap classrooms'.
These were red cedar huts
with large windows and
wide doors which opened
out on to verandas in
marked comfort to the
traditional architecture
seen in this picture.*

Fig. 113

*During the Second World
War some nationals from
Nazi-occupied countries
managed to escape to
Scotland, from where they
attempted to help free
their homelands. They
included a number of
Polish soldiers, who
formed an ambulance unit
based in Linlithgow at
what is now Laetare
International Youth
Hostel. Here a Scottish
ATS recruit is seen
working on one of the
vehicles which the Poles
used to provide a service
throughout the Forth
valley.*

Fig. 114

Opposite. *The entry of the
United States into the war
brought the Yanks to
Scotland, among them
these sailors, who enjoyed
pints of beer with their
British counterparts at
Rosyth. While petrol
rationing still made travel
difficult, many of the
Americans managed to
find ways of reaching
Edinburgh, where they
helped to enliven the
night-life of the city.*

cities, the 'Land Girls', as they were nicknamed, were either billeted at the
farms where they worked or were provided with accommodation nearby in
large private homes, such as at Saltoun Hall and Eaglescairnie, the Salvesen
shipping line family's spacious home in East Lothian, which were requisitioned for that purpose. Despite long hard hours of manual labour in the
fields, from sewing seeds to harvesting the resultant crops, the Land Girls still
also managed to establish a reputation for being able to party in the evenings
and at weekends at dances such as those held by the 'Brylcream Boys' at air
bases in Donibristle in Fife and Macmerry in East Lothian.

On social occasions such as these, however, the British lads did not have
it all their own way because they faced opposition from foreign rivals –
Belgians, Poles and Norwegians during the early years of the war and later,
after the USA entered the fray following the Japanese attack on Pearl
Harbour, from American airmen who were based at East Fortune. While
dozens of Lothian girls began GI brides, hundreds of others fell in love with
the immaculately mannered, smartly uniformed Poles, who had camps in
Haddington and Gifford in East Lothian, where the men of their Armoured

Division, the 10th Mounted Rifles were based, and at Dalmeny and Linlithgow in West Lothian, where their ambulance corp had its head-quarters.

After peace returned in May 1945 many of the Poles did not return to their native country but chose to stay on in the east of Scotland, and Polish surnames are now common in Edinburgh and most towns throughout the Forth Valley. The Poles also left several memorials, including the stained glass windows in the apse of the little Norman church at Dalmeny, and the shrine to the Virgin Mary in the courtyard of their former camp at Linlithgow. Their Linlithgow camp is now the premises of Laetare International Youth Camp, which continues its role of international cooperation in encouraging young people from all over the world to get together and gain an understanding of different cultures and countries.

GRANGEMOUTH AERODROME

Further up the Forth at Grangemouth, the new Central Scotland Aerodrome, which had only commenced passenger flights in May 1939, was also requisitioned by the RAF as a training base. Since May, the new airfield had already been used by members of the newly-formed Royal Airforce Volunteer Training Reserve, and the first Commanding Officer at Grangemouth was Captain D.V. Carnegie, who went on to become Air Marshall Commanding New Zealand Air Force. Amongst the planes based at Grangemouth during the early months of the war were Blenheims, Defiants, Gladiators, Lysanders, Spitfires and Whirlwinds. The Defiants were very distinctive and easily identifiable by their revolving gun turrets. Occasionally the Fleet Air Arm from Donibristle, near what is now the new town of Dalgety Bay on the Fife shore, used the grass strip at Grangemouth to simulate deck landings in their naval Swordfish.

In October 1940, Grangemouth was transferred to RAF Fighter Command and became part of Number 81 Training Group. It soon became recognised as a finishing-school for young pilots from the British Commonwealth as well as from Poland and all parts of the United Kingdom. Wing Commander H.A.V. Hogan, who later became Air Vice Marshall, was appointed Chief Flying Instructor. The training took place initially using the famous Spitfires and two lesser-known types of aircraft, Fairy Battles and Masters. Flying Officer B.J.C. Cadbury from City of Edinburgh Squadron was drafted in to inform the young pilots about the tactics of the Luftwaffe.

The recreation hall at the Scottish Oil Refinery on the shores of the Forth

opposite the aerodrome became the Sergeants' Mess, while Weedinghall
mansion near Polmont was utilised as billets for most of the single officers.
Other ranks were accommodated in the recently built primary school at
Westquarter.

The Fighter Operational Training Unit at Grangemouth was officially
known as No. 58 OTU, and on 21 January 1941 it received an official visit
from HRH Group Captain the Duke of Kent, in his capacity as a Fighter
Command Welfare Officer. Amongst the unit's most famous trainees was
Pilot Officer Neville Duke. Other well-known names connected with
Grangemouth Aerodrome were Ralph Reader of Scout Gang Show fame,
who presented one of his earliest concerts there, and Max Bygraves, who
entertained his fellow airmen at the base at a concert in the local Town Hall,
long before he went on to become one of the country's top comedians.

By the summer of 1941, the enrolment of trainee pilots at Grangemouth
had become even more international, with recruits from Czechoslovakia, the
Netherlands and the United States. The American airmen were the first to be
trained in Great Britain. In August one of the new American pilots, R.F.
Minnock, was killed when his Spitfire hit another during a mock dog-fight.
His plane dived out of control and he failed to bale out before it hit the
ground.

The first women to be posted to Grangemouth arrived in March 1942,
when twenty-eight WAAFs took up residence. They were soon followed by a
further twenty-two women, who were trained as flight mechanics.
Operations at Grangemouth were hampered in November when a severe
blaze swept through the station headquarters and control tower. However,
temporary arrangements were made to continue pilot training. Other fighter
aces who graduated from the Grangemouth school included the future Air
Marshall Stapleton, Rhodesian E.P.W. Bocock, who went on to command
No. 602 City of Glasgow Squadron, Canadian R.W. McNair, and P.L.
Arnott, who was awarded the DFC and Bar.

Back on the river the hostilities brought an enormous increase in the
work force at Rosyth, which became Scotland's largest wartime employer
with 8,000 men and 2,000 women on its books. Most worked twelve-hour
shifts, and between 1939 and 1945 they were responsible for repairing over
3,000 ships. The log for the Royal Naval Dockyard for these years includes
many interesting incidents, starting as early as October 1939, when the
Polish submarine *Orzel*, which had succeeded in escaping the German
invasion, arrived at the port. One month later top secrecy was imposed when
HMS *Belfast* was towed in after breaking her back when she struck a mine in
the North Sea.

All was not doom and gloom, however, and industries along the shores of the Forth quickly geared up to help the war effort. Upriver at Alloa docks many motor torpedo-boats were constructed; at Thomson and Balfour's Timber Yard at Bridgeness near Bo'ness workers capitalised on their woodworking skills to build wooden-hulled mine-sweepers; further down the Firth at Burntisland the shipbuilding yard converted from its peace-time role of building small cargo vessels to constructing several small auxiliary aircraft carriers. These small carriers were specially built to act as escorts to convoys crossing the North Atlantic and, as well as providing air cover to guard the other ships, were cleverly designed below the flight deck to transport much-needed cargoes of grain to ease the bread rationing in wartime Britain. A cut-away model showing the interior of one of these ingenious vessels, the *Empire MacKendrick*, is on display in Burntisland Museum.

WARTIME ROYAL VISIT

Scotland received a morale-boosting visit from King George VI and Queen Elizabeth on 26 February 1940. The popular royal couple toured Leith Docks, which eight days earlier had been congratulated by the First Lord of the Admiralty, Sir Winston Churchill, for the efficient way in which it had handled the British prisoners of war who had been rescued from the *Altmark* and landed there by HMS *Cossack*. The king and queen included in their tour a visit to the shipbuilding yard of Henry Robb, whose workers were doing sterling wartime work. In her book *The Port of Leith*, Sue Mowat reports that during the Second World War Robbs built forty-two naval and fourteen merchant ships, and repaired or refitted 3,000 vessels. These figures represent one new ship every six weeks and one repaired every day of the war. At the start of the war Robbs was ordered by the Admiralty to build Flower class corvettes. The first four, HMS *Delphinium*, HMS *Dianthus*, HMS *Petunia* and HMS *Polyanthus*, were launched in 1940, with HMS *Lotus* and HMS *Pink* following in 1942. That same year Robbs also launched HMS *Ness* and HMS *Nith*, the first two of twelve frigates which it constructed. In 1943 it switched to the production of Castle class frigates and that year and the next HMS *Flint Castle*, HMS *Hespeler* and HMS *Orangeville* all took to the water at the busy Leith yard. During this hectic period Robbs also constructed two wooden-hulled mine-sweepers, named HMS *Sidmouth* and HMS *Stornoway*, as well as three mine-sweeping

Fig. 116

Photograph taken during George VI's visit to Rosyth on 6 March 1941.

Fig. 117

King George VI paused to speak to the Pipe Major of the Black Watch, who played him aboard HMS King George V during his 1941 visit to the battle-ship named after his father.

Fig. 118

The censor again insisted in blacking out the background to this photograph taken as King George VI boarded HMS King George V during visit to Rosyth in 1941.

training vessels for the New Zealand Government. All of this effort was again recognised when, on 29 July 1943, Henry Robbs was honoured with a second visit from the king and queen.

Fig. 119

The canteen at Rosyth offered the comfort of a cup of tea and sticky buns to these off-duty sailors during a run ashore. The mural which ran around the canteen made an interesting background.

ROSYTH

In March 1940 there was strict security when the mighty newly built battleship which bore the name of his majesty's father, the 35,000-ton HMS *King George V*, arrived at Rosyth for fitting out. Her armour-plated hull had a thickness at the water line of sixteen inches, and once work on her was completed in the following December, she played a leading role in many major missions. These included transporting Britain's new ambassador to the United States, Lord Halifax, to New York in January 1941, protecting North Atlantic and Arctic convoys, taking part in the hunt for the *Bismarck* and, later, leading the British Pacific Task Force. After the war her career continued until 1957, when she was scrapped. As work continued on *King George V*, Rosyth experienced one of its busiest periods of the whole war. In April 1940, 1,200 vessels assembled in the Forth prior to the Norwegian campaign against the German occupying forces.

The world's largest warship, the 42,000-ton battle-cruiser HMS *Hood*, was that summer refitted at Rosyth. The 'Mighty *Hood*', as she was known, was a much older vessel than the *King George V*, her construction dating from the First World War, and she was actually due for a major refit. But the pressures of war meant that there was insufficient time to allow for this. The hull of the *Hood* had been laid at John Brown's Shipyard at Clydebank in September 1916, and she was launched in August 1918 at the then enormous cost of £6,000,000 – the equivalent of £146 per ton. Fitting-out then took a further two years, and she did not come into service until 1920. The *Hood*, 860 feet long, and with a beam of 105 feet, is said to have loomed over the whole of Rosyth during her months in the port. Her main armament of eight fifteen-inch six-ton guns, together with her secondary armament of twelve five-point five-inch guns, each twenty-three feet long and capable of firing shells weighing up to eighty-five pounds, made her the most formidable of opponents. It was disastrous for the British war effort, after all the work of her refit at Rosyth, when she was sunk in the Denmark Strait east of Greenland only months later, on 23 May 1941. She was lost in action against the German flagship, *Bismarck*, whose shells hit her below the armour-plated belt which surrounded her hull. As the shells from the *Bismarck* found their target, there was a massive explosion, probably in her munitions store, and

Fig. 120

Top. *A lone sailor seeking a moment of peace and quiet in the Chapel of St Andrew at Rosyth.*

Fig. 121

Bottom. *Another moment of silent contemplation at Rosyth during the Second World War. Beyond the solitary dock labourer the cranes of the Royal Naval Dockyard are visible.*

Fig. 122

Opposite. *Tugs carefully guide the massive battleship HMS* Duke of York *into Rosyth.*

Fig. 123
HMS Duke of York displayed the full might of her powerful fourteen-inch guns as she was manoeuvred into Rosyth by her attendant tugs.

Fig. 124

*This unusual view of HMS
Duke of York in dock at
Rosyth was taken from
the top of the Royal Naval
Dockyard's eighty-foot-
high crane.*

Fig. 125
HMS *Duke of York and
her city class companion
HMS* Liverpool.

Fig. 126
*The mighty armaments of
HMS Duke of York are
clearly seen in this
photograph of the bows of
the vessel, taken while she
was in dry dock at Rosyth.*

Fig. 129

Top. *Tugs guarding the aircraft carrier HMS ? as she entered the Royal Naval Dockyard.*

Fig. 130

Bottom. *During his visit to the Royal Naval Dockyard at Rosyth, Prime Minister Churchill boarded HMS* King George V *and is seen here addressing the ship's company on the fore-deck of the mighty vessel.*

Fig. 131

Opposite. *This photograph was taken from one of the huge cranes at Rosyth during the refit of the battleship* King George V.

Fig. 132

Top. *Wearing his naval cap, Winston Churchill was photographed as he descended the gangway after his speech aboard* HMS King George V.

Fig. 133

Bottom. *The wheel-house and bridge of the battleship* HMS King George V *loomed over her forward guns. The cranes of the Royal Naval Dockyard are visible in the background.*

Fig. 134

Opposite. *The hull of* King George V *soared skyward above the outline of the dry dock at Rosyth.*

Fig. 135
The 'Mighty' HMS Hood, the largest warship of the time, sailing through the boom defence away from the Royal Naval Dockyard at Rosyth after a quick partial refit in 1940. Only weeks later she was sunk by the German battleship Bismarck and all but three of her crew died in the icy waters off the coast of Greenland.

Fig. 136

The battle-cruiser HMS Repulse was scheduled to take King George VI and Queen Elizabeth on a royal tour of Canada when the outbreak of the Second World War necessitated the cancellation of this plan. She sailed instead for the Far East where, on 10 December 1941, she was attacked and sunk by Japanese bombers off Singapore. The battleship HMS Prince of Wales was lost in the same attack, and the combined loss of life was 790 members of their ships' companies.

the *Hood* sank swiftly with the loss of all but three of her crew of 1,419 men. It was a tragedy.

Despite such a setback, work at Rosyth continued. HMS *Cossack* was completely fitted out and the battleship HMS *Queen Elizabeth* arrived from Portsmouth to complete her modernisation programme. An interesting story about HMS *Queen Elizabeth*, much related in the pubs of Rosyth and the surrounding area at this time, told how the battleship, prior to her arrival at the dockyard, had passed the famous Cunard passenger liner of the same name in mid-Atlantic as the latter made her high-speed top-secret dash in the opposite direction for conversion into a vitally required troopship. Strict radio silence was in force, but it was claimed that the commander of HMS *Queen Elizabeth* ordered his radio officer to breach it momentarily to transmit the Morse code message which spelt out the single word 'Snap!'

HMS *Queen Elizabeth* was followed to Rosyth by the new battleship HMS *Prince of Wales*, which had only been commissioned in March 1941, but already required repairs. Back at sea, she soon afterwards had the honour of avenging the sinking of the *Hood* when, along with HMS *King George V* and her fellow battleship, HMS *Rodney*, they succeeded in hunting down the *Bismarck* and sending her to the bottom on 27 May 1941. Sadly, soon afterwards, a similar fate awaited the *Prince of Wales*. In December

1941, off Singapore, she was attacked by eighty-eight Japanese bombers and torpedo-planes and sunk. The battle-cruiser HMS *Repulse* was also sunk in the same attack and, together, the two ships lost 730 men.

With such enormous losses being sustained, the British government felt it was imperative to do everything possible to maintain the morale of ships' crews while they were in port, and so the services' entertainment unit, ENSA, staged a series of concerts at the Royal Naval Dockyard. According to many servicemen, ENSA meant 'Every Night Something Awful', but not apparently at Rosyth, where amongst those who appeared were stars of British entertainment, including singer Gracie Fields and actresses Evelyn Laye and Beatrice Lilie. On 6 March 1941 Rosyth was also honoured by a royal visit from King George VI, who travelled north from London by royal train for the occasion. The king also sailed across the Forth to Port Edgar to see minesweeper training taking place at HMS *Lochinvar*, which was the main base for such work in Britain, with some of the exercises also taking place further downriver at Granton Harbour.

PORT EDGAR

Port Edgar, which derives its name from Prince Edgar Ethling, the brother of Queen Margaret (after whom the neighbouring burgh of Queensferry on the south shore of the Forth is named), was originally a coal-bunkering and ferry port. It was first purchased by the Admiralty during the First World War, and opened as a naval base in 1916. By the following year it was home port for sixty-six destroyers, with total crews of over 5,000, and 1,000 civilian staff. Barracks and a naval hospital were built nearby at Butlaw. In 1927 Port Edgar was reduced to a care and maintenance basis and, during the depression years at the beginning of the 1930s, some of the disused barracks were temporarily reopened as a summer holiday camp for unemployed families from Edinburgh and Glasgow. Several school camps were also held – a use which was suggested again in the 1980s for the building known as the Norwegian Block.

In 1939 Port Edgar was hurriedly re-commissioned as a land-based training school, known as HMS *Lochinvar*, for the training of mine-sweeper crews. As the Royal Navy's only facility dedicated to this work, Port Edgar was also used as the sea base for the testing of all new mine-disposal gear. In the space of six years, 13,000 ratings and 4,000 officers passed through HMS *Lochinvar*, and at any one time there were as many as 6,000 men stationed there.

The most famous of those trained at HMS *Lochinvar* was the exiled
Prince Olaf, Crown Prince of Norway. Together with fellow Norwegian
officers who had succeeded in escaping the German occupation of their own
country, he was billeted in Queensferry Burgh Chambers, whose distinctive
premises in Queensferry High Street had begun life as a hotel, with
magnificent views straight out across the Forth. It was in the former hotel
sitting-room that, each Christmas during their stay, a little Christmas tree was
erected and decorated. The trees were brought all the way across the North
Sea from Norway by the famous Shetland Bus, the informal transport system
which succeeded in keeping contact between Scotland and Scandinavia
throughout the war years. Norway has never forgotten the hospitality which
was extended to its future king during his stay in Scotland, and, to this day, a
tall Norwegian fir tree is felled and shipped to Edinburgh every Christmas,
where it takes pride of place on the Mound, overlooking Princes Street.

As well as Prince Olaf and his Norwegian colleagues, HMS *Lochinvar*
also trained many exiled Belgian seamen, who had also succeeded in fleeing
the advancing Germans. But the sailors who came from furthest away to Port
Edgar sailed there all the way from the Falkland Islands in the South
Atlantic, making the 8,000-mile journey in their own fishing trawler.

All this naval activity at Port Edgar meant, as it had done during the First
World War, a very prosperous time for the pubs and cafes in nearby
Queensferry, where was also located the new attraction of the Art Deco-style
Rio Cinema, which the sailors nicknamed the 'R Ten'. To cope with the
demand for entertainment from the navy men, film programmes were
changed three times a week. Instead of the first and second houses of pre-war
days, continuous showings were introduced, which meant that patrons often
came in the middle of the big film. But it is said the sailors never grumbled,
being too busily occupied with their girlfriends even to notice. After the
pictures and the pubs closed at ten o'clock, trouble often flared up in
Queensferry's long, narrow cobbled High Street. The burgh's police force was
increased to eight, but, especially on Friday and Saturday nights, they often
had to call on the Red Caps of the naval base's shore patrol to help defuse
situations which often became as explosive as any minefield.

MERCHANT CASUALTIES

According to the *Shipwreck Index of the British Isles*, mention of mines is a
reminder that the war also affected merchant shipping on the Forth. The first
casualty of the Second World War in the Forth was the Norwegian-owned

Fig. 137
*After spending the Second
World War in exile in
Scotland, with his
headquarters at what is
now the museum in
Queensferry High Street,
Crown Prince Olav of
Norway finally returned to
his homeland in 1945.
Here he is seen boarding
HMS Apollo for the
voyage back across the
North Sea.*

Fig. 138
Travelling in the opposite direction were these German officers. Here thay are shown arriving at Drem, East Lothian, preparing to hand over details of German minefields and defences along the Norwegian coast.

Fig. 139
Naval ratings march
through the streets of the
historic burgh of
Inverkeithing, near North
Queensferry in Fife.

Fig. 140

The parade was attended by Provost Binny, who sported his gold chain of office for the occasion.

cargo vessel *Arcturus*, attacked and torpedoed by *U21* on 1 December 1939. The following day, the cargo ship *Rudolf*, which was registered in neutral Sweden, hit a mine and sank off St Abbs Head. Scandinavian casualties continued later in the month when, on 17 December, the Danish-owned cargo ship *Bogo* sank off Fife Ness while en route for Methil.

Four days before Christmas 1939, at 3 p.m., the whole of Leith Docks was shaken by a huge explosion when the small boom-defence vessel *Bayonet* blew up. Planes of City of Edinburgh Squadron, based at Drem, were immediately scrambled to search for suspected German bombers. There were none, and it was later concluded that the *Bayonet* had not been bombed by the enemy, but had probably been destroyed by a mine. However, as the RAF Spitfires from Drem patrolled over the Forth, their pilots did spot two bombers over the river and succeeded in shooting down one of them. Unfortunately, they then realised that they were both British Hampdens. The plane which was hit crashed into the Forth off Gullane.

There was then a lull in enemy action in the Forth estuary until 3 February 1940, when the Norwegian cargo steamer *Tempo* was bombed by a German raider off St Abbs Head. A second casualty on the 24th of that month was the British-registered *Royal Archer*, which, while on passage from

London to Leith, hit a mine off Inchkeith island. The crew and one passenger succeeded in abandoning ship before she sank. They were picked up by the trawler *Tourmaline* and landed at Leith. Three days later another of the Forth fishing fleet, the trawler *Ben Attow*, herself became a casualty when she hit a mine off the May Island and sank.

One of the worst losses of the war occurred on 27 July when the SS *Salvestria*, having sailed safely all the way from the southern tip of South America, strayed from the swept channel on her approach to Leith and detonated an acoustic mine which had been dropped by a German aircraft. As her name indicated, the *Salvestria* belonged to Christian Salvesen of Leith, but she was originally the passenger liner *Cardiganshire*. Built in 1913, she was capable then of carrying just over 1,000 passengers. When her days as an ocean liner were over, she was purchased by Salvesen, who converted her into a factory ship to service their fleet of steam whale-catchers operating in the Antarctic. Later she was converted again, this time into a mobile oil-refinery to process the oil obtained from whale blubber. It was while bringing a cargo of this vitally-needed commodity back to Scotland that she was lost off the island of Inchkeith, within sight of her home-port and final destination, Leith.

Later in the year a second vessel which had, like the *Salvestria*, successfully survived the First World War to make a contribution to the Second, the veteran Admiralty tug *Saucy*, also hit a mine on 4 October, again off Inchkeith.

Christian Salvesen was not the only Leith ship-owner to lose a vessel during this period of the war. Off Dunbar on 15 October 1940 the Gibson Line vessel *Halland*, which had been requisitioned for the duration of the hostilities by the Ministry of Transport, was attacked from the air. She was badly hit and sank quickly, possibly because of the heavy cargo of bagged cement in her holds.

Later the same month, on 10 October, on the opposite side of the river, the Dutch-registered cargo vessel *Arizona* went down when she hit a mine off Elie Ness. Twelve days later, another mine put paid to the fishing boat *Girl Mary*, which had been requisitioned by the Royal Navy. She sank off the island of Inchcolm. A further fishing boat was lost on 27 October when the *Persevere*, which was serving as an Admiralty armed patrol-vessel, also hit a mine in the river. Fishing industry casualties continued on 2 November when a mine destroyed yet another fishing boat, the *Goodwill*.

On 22 November 1940 the steam lighter *Glen*, which was carrying a cargo of ammunition, was attacked by the Germans from the air off Rosyth and sank near the Royal Navy Ammunition Supply Depot at Crombie Point. The following day the Royal Navy lost a second small vessel when the motor

Leith
Trockendocks (Innenhafen)

Karte 1:100 000
Blatt
Sch 27

1:63 360
Blatt
Sch 68

Kriegsaufnahme:
596 R 5f

Länge(west.Greenw.):3 °10′0″, Breite:55°58′45″(Bildmitte)
Mißweisung -13°30′(Mitte 1938), Zielhöhe über NN 10 m

Nachträge:
2.10.39.

Maßstab etwa 1: 14 500   (1cm → 145 m)

Ⓐ   GB 83 77 Trockendocks (Außenhafen)

1) 4 Trockendocks, Länge v.90-170m, Breite v.20-25m
2) 6 Werkstatt-u.Betriebsgebäude   etwa 1 700 qm
   bebaute Fläche(Schwerpunkte)   etwa 1 700 qm
   Gleisanschluß vorhanden

Ⓑ   GB 83 84 Trockendocks (Innenhafen)

1) 4 Trockendocks, Länge v.46-85m, Breite v.14-20m
2) 10 Werkstatt-u.Betriebsgebäude   etwa 3 400 qm
   bebaute Fläche(Schwerpunkte)   etwa 3 400 qm

   Gleisanschluß nicht vorhanden

[172]

launch *Good Design* hit a mine while sailing past Inchkeith Island. The explosion was so severe that the hull of the little craft was blown in two and two of her six crew were killed in the blast.

Two days after Christmas 1940 the trawler *Ben Gulvain*, which was on mine-sweeping duties for the Admiralty, detonated a mine, once again off Inchkeith. She survived the blast and, after repairs, continued in service until 1946.

Fig. 141
A German aerial photograph of the port of Leith taken in October 1939.

The first loss of the following year was on 7 March, when the Norwegian-registered *Einar Jarl* sank off Fife Ness when she hit a mine. She was sailing light without any cargo in her holds, en route from Hull to the Canadian port of Halifax in Nova Scotia.

The next month, on 2 April, the Grimsby-registered fishing trawler *Fortuna*, which had been chartered by the Royal Navy, was caught in a friendly-fire incident off St Abbs Head, accidentally shelled and sunk by RAF fighters. Two of her crew died in the incident. On the same day the Leith trawler *Cramond Island*, which had done duty for the Admiralty as a boom-defence vessel since the outbreak of the war in 1939, also sank in the same waters.

Another major war casualty occurred on 3 June when the passenger vessel *Royal Fusilier*, belonging to the London–Edinburgh Steamship Company Ltd, was bombed off the Bass Rock while on passage from London to Leith. The passenger service had been suspended since the start of the war, and she was sailing as a cargo ship, with a large quantity of paper and rice in her holds. There was no loss of life.

German JU 88 fighters carried out a daring raid on the trawler *Cradock* on 8 November 1941 and sank her while she was sailing off St Abbs Head. The year ended with an unfortunate incident when the Admiralty-built armed patrol-vessel *Boy Andrew* was in collision with the Northern Isles steamer *St Rognvald* in the narrow channel which had been swept for mines off Inchkeith. The *Boy Andrew* was so badly holed that she subsequently sank.

There was a marked decrease in enemy action during 1942, thanks to the increased presence of the Royal Navy and the introduction of convoys with armed protection, which made German U-boats and planes much more wary of attacking. But then in December, after eleven months with no losses, another of the Aberdeen-owned Ben trawlers, the *Ben Screel*, hit a mine and sank off St Abbs Head.

Royal Navy and RAF cover was also very effective during 1943, when no ships were lost to enemy action. The only casualty occurred at the very end of the year when, on 22 December, there was an explosion aboard the barge *BV 42* in Leith Docks.

The following year also began well, but on 2 April 1944 there was a tragic incident when, during an exercise in Aberlady Bay, two landing craft, *LCA 845* and *LCA 811*, both foundered while practising beach landings in preparation for the D-Day invasion of Europe later in the summer. Both vessels were heavily armed with twenty-four mortars, set in four rows of six weapons fore and aft, whose spiky appearance had earned these small craft the nickname of 'hedgehogs'.

The navy suffered another loss in the Forth on 27 October 1944: the former destroyer, HMS *Rockingham*, which had been acquired from the Americans under the 1940 Lease-Lend Act. After her conversion into an aircraft practice-target vessel earlier that year, she sank after hitting a mine off Fife Ness.

Although the Allies were by then confident that the war was almost over, there was at the start of 1945 a marked increase in German submarine activity around the entrance to the Firth of Forth. The British-registered cargo vessel SS *Egholm* was attacked while sailing in convoy off St Abbs Head on 25 February, and torpedoed and sunk by *U2322*. The following month the Royal Navy had its revenge when another U-boat, *U714*, was detected, depth-charged and destroyed with all hands by the destroyer HMS *Wyvern* and the South African naval frigate *Natal*.

This deadly game of tit-for-tat continued on 5 April when, while sailing light from Grangemouth to Blythe in Northumberland to pick up cargo, the cargo vessel SS *Gasray* was torpedoed and sunk by *U978*. Six of the *Gasray's* crew were killed.

The terrible futility of war was never more apparent than on 7 May 1945, when the Norwegian cargo vessel SS *Sneland* became the last vessel to be torpedoed during the Second World War. She was attacked and sunk off the May Island during the final hour of the conflict by *U2336* under the command of Captain Emil Klusemeir, who was on his first patrol as skipper of a submarine. Six of the *Sneland's* crew were killed, but *U2336* had not finished her deadly work. After the war in Europe was officially over – after the German surrender had been signalled but before the cease fire took effect – Captain Klusemeir ordered his crew to launch one last attack, again in the waters off the May Island. This time the attack was on the British cargo ship *Avondale Park*, which was sailing from Hull to Belfast via the Pentland Firth in order to avoid the dangers of the English Channel. At 11 p.m. the torpedo from the *U2336* struck its target. The *Avondale Park* sank and her wreck still lies off the Isle of May, where it is a favourite site for local divers. When he returned from his first and last patrol as a U-boat commander, Captain Klusemeir, vehemently denied receiving the signal sent to all U-boats by the German High Command instructing them to cease hostilities.

THE MULBERRY HARBOUR

Almost from the time of the evacuation of British troops from Dunkirk, plans were made for their eventual return to the continent. The major problem was that the enemy had so heavily defended every possible port on the shores of northern France, of Belgium and of Holland that the military authorities realised that it would be almost impossible to capture any one of them for use as a military bridgehead. The only feasible solution, strongly supported by Winston Churchill, was to design and construct an entire floating harbour. In pursuit of this ambitious aim, trials of several prototypes took place at Garlieston in Wigtonshire in the far south-west of Scotland. The outcome was the decision to build not just one but two Mulberry Harbours, one for the British landings and the other for the use of the American forces, who had by this time entered the war under General Eisenhower. Thus it was that, shortly before Christmas 1943, many of the employees at Henry Robb's Shipbuilding Yard at Leith suddenly found themselves switched from building naval vessels to work on this top-secret project.

So large was the project that an entirely new construction yard was hurriedly built on the flat land near the western extension to the docks, which had only recently been reclaimed from the Forth. Shifts of men and women worked around the clock over both the Christmas and New Year holidays to complete the new construction facility, which was equipped with prefabricated sheds and offices as well as heavy lifting cranes and slipways. By the beginning of 1944 work on the first section of Mulberry was underway, and the first floating pier-head was launched on 26 January. A second of the strange looking 'Hippos' (as they were nicknamed) was completed in February, and a third took to the water on 11 March. Even this impressive rate of work was, however, not sufficient if Mulberry was to be finished in time for the Normandy landings to take place as planned in June.

Alexander Findlay and Co. of Motherwell had designed the units and were in charge of co-ordinating the work, which involved over 100 Scottish firms, from Cairnryan on the west coast to Leith in the east. They demanded that the employees seconded by Robb increase their output to complete one pier-head every week. The Leith workers rose to the challenge, although they were still unaware of how important their task was or how the results of their efforts were to change the future of the war.

As soon as each Hippo was launched, it was towed from Leith the short distance upriver to Newhaven, where it was berthed alongside the fish quay (where the museum and Harry Ramsdens fish restaurant are now situated).

Fig. 142

Top. *Two pierheads for the Mulberry harbour were photographed after their launch at Leith.*

Fig. 143

Bottom. *Work on spud pontoons at Alex Findley's yard, Leith, for subsequent use as vital components of the Mulberry harbours off the coast of Normandy, France in June 1944.*

There finishing-work took place. The Leith workforce of 600 men and women built thirteen pier-heads and sixteen large pontoons in total, and all were completed on time.

Several of the powerful sea-going tugs for whose construction the yard of Henry Robb was particularly famed towed the flotilla of Mulberry components from the Forth to the south coast of England. On 6 June 1944, the Leith-built tugs were among the 300 which crossed the Channel during the hours of darkness and helped put together the huge floating jigsaw puzzles which became Mulberry A and Mulberry B. By dawn the D-Day landings were underway and the beginning of the end of the war was in sight.

THE FORTH AT PEACE

Peace in Europe came in May 1945, and the vital role Roysth had played in the war effort was marked five months later when King George VI, Queen Elizabeth and the young Princess Margaret Rose travelled north by royal train to the Royal Naval Dockyard on 29 September to conduct an investiture aboard the aircraft carrier HMS *Implacable*. This was His Majesty's first visit to his fleet since the end of the war and, accompanied by Admiral Sir Henry R. Moore, Commander in Chief, Home Fleet, the royal party also boarded the 30,900-ton battleship HMS *Rodney*. Wearing three strings of pearls and with a fox fur hung over her left arm, the queen paused to chat to Captain R.O. Fitzroy and Commander R. Jones as she reached the top of the gangway, then boarded the great ship, whose deck was 710 feet long and 106 feet broad. Built by Cammel Laird and completed in August 1927 at a cost of over £7,000,000, *Rodney* was a sister ship to HMS *Nelson* and, by then, one of the Royal Navy's older vessels, whose service years had been prolonged by the hostilities. She had a service speed of twenty-three knots and a wartime complement of 1,640 officers and men.

Although Rosyth's important contribution to the war was thus clearly recognised, its future was uncertain. As after the First World War, for Rosyth peace meant a huge reduction in work and the workers required to carry it out. Fortunately, the end of hostilities also again meant a very busy time for the ship-breaking industry, and many of the dockyard's former employees found work with Thomas W. Ward of Inverkeithing, which, now that Metal Industries had relocated to a larger site at Faslane, on the River Clyde, dominated the scrap scene on the Forth.

The Admiralty, faced with the need to create a greatly scaled-down

Fig. 144
Following V.E. Day on 8 May 1945, many German merchant ships were impounded and laid up in Methil Bay, as seen in this aerial photograph taken on 28 June 1945.

Fig. 145

With her sixteen-inch guns, HMS Nelson, *along with her sister ship HMS* Rodney, *had the most powerful armaments of any British naval vessel during the Second World War. Launched in 1927, she cost £6,400,000, and was broken up by Wards of Inverkeithing in 1948.*

peacetime Royal Navy, divided the existing fleet into three categories: refit, reserve and scrap. During the years which followed, the battleships HMS *Royal Sovereign*, HMS *Howe* and HMS *Revenge*, together with the aircraft carrier, HMS *Formidable* (built in 1940 and active as part of the British Pacific Fleet in the Far East), all came under the breakers' hammers at Rosyth and Inverkeithing. All of these vessels had proud war records, but now that the world was again at peace there was no room for sentiment. There was a huge demand for the scrap which their hulls yielded to help with rebuilding post-war Britain.

HMS *Howe* was a ship with particularly strong Scottish connections. One of four battleships built in the King George V class she was built on the Clyde by Fairfield Engineering and Shipbuilding Company of Govan. Work on her massive hull was begun in June 1937 and was completed in May 1942. One of HMS *Howe*'s last duties before being placed in the Reserve Fleet and finally scapped, was to take part in the naval review held in the estuary of the River Clyde in July 1947, when, despite atrocious weather conditions ranging from dense fog to a torrential thunderstorm, His Majesty King George VI and Queen Elizabeth came to the Tail of the Bank at Greenock to sail out and inspect the Home Fleet.

The large naval vessels, the scrapping of which kept the Forth ship breakers busy for many months, were also accompanied by many smaller destroyers and frigates, and later the American navy's heavy cruiser USS *St Helena*. It is about this latter vessel that a famous tale is told. Instead of ringing finished with engines for the last time and waiting to be towed to her final berth in Rosyth, she is reputed to have continued to sail steadily on upriver. When he received a frantic radio message demanding to know why he was still sailing on, the American captain is alleged to have replied, 'But I was ordered to drop anchor after the fourth bridge and so far I've only sailed under one!'

(Mention of sailing below the Forth Bridge also recalls the tradition which demands that if a train crosses over while a Royal Navy vessel is passing beneath, the navigating officer has to stand drinks all round in the officers' wardroom. If two trains cross the bridge in opposite directions while a Royal Navy ship sails under the bridge the price to pay is even higher: the custom is that the captain must buy a round for the entire ship's company.)

Had the skipper of the American cruiser not heeded the radio message he might very well have found a final resting-place for his ship further up the Forth. In addition to the scrapping work being carried out by Wards at Inverkeithing and Rosyth, many smaller naval vessels were also broken up at the Bridgeness and Carriden yards near Bo'ness, which were operated by P. and W. McLellan. During 1946 the Bridgeness yard also disposed of several redundant submarines which, while they awaited their end, were temporarily beached on the mud-banks a short distance further upriver in Kinneil Bay, between Bo'ness and Grangemouth.

During the war years commercial trade had continued on a limited scale at Grangemouth, but Bo'ness was entirely requisitioned by the Admiralty and closed to merchant shipping for the duration of hostilities. Its dock became a base for mine-sweepers, landing craft and other small vessels, which were kept in a good state of repair by the employees of Cochrane's Engineering Works, whose premises overlooked the docks just as in the First World War. Bill Cochrane, the present senior member of the family, recalls how the commanding officer at Bo'ness invited his father to accompany him on a visit to Rosyth to be introduced to his superior, Admiral Bovell, only to discover to his surprise upon their arrival that the two men were already on first-name terms. Bovell had served as a junior officer at Bo'ness twenty-five years before, during the earlier conflict with Germany!

The shore depot at Bo'ness was named HMS *Stopford*, and the hosiery at the East Bog in the town became its main base. Many of the large Victorian villas overlooking the Forth, which had been built by well-to-do Bo'ness

Fig. 146
Further up the Forth, many naval vessels met their ends at P. and W. McLellan's ship-breaking yards at Bridgeness and Carriden on the south shore of the river. Here a destroyer and a submarine both come under the breakers' hammers at the Bridgeness Yard. The sawmill belonging to Thomson and Balfour, where small naval craft, such as motor torpedo boats, were constructed with wooden hulls during the Second War can also be seen on the landward side of the harbour.

Fig. 147

When the Royal Navy took over exclusive use of Bo'ness harbour and dock, it requisitioned Tidings Hill, the home of the Denholm family, as its headquarters in the old town.

merchants and ship-owners, were requisitioned to house officers, while others were billeted in the homes of local families. Stopford's senior officers made their headquarters at Tidings Hill, in Cadzow Crescent, the mansion-house owned by the well-known ship-owning family, the Denholms, whose son George was at the time leading the RAF's City of Edinburgh Squadron of Spitfires. The big house overlooking the harbour and the docks was so named because it was there that, in the nineteenth century, wives and sweethearts gathered to catch their first glimpse each autumn of the returning Bo'ness Arctic whaling fleet. Its past reputation as a place to which sailors returned safely was looked upon as a good omen by the officers who occupied it during the Second World War. At the other end of Bo'ness, in the town's tree-lined Grahamsdyke Road, Rosyth House (now a bed and breakfast) housed the Wrens attached to HMS *Stopford*. It is still known to older inhabitants of Bo'ness as the 'Wrenery'.

Back down-river at Rosyth, the remaining workers at the Royal Naval Dockyard received a boost on 1 July 1946 when an oil tanker was accepted for commercial refit. Soon afterwards, in August, more work arrived for Wards when HMS *Implacable* sailed in to be scrapped.

Wards purchased three further naval vessels for scrapping in 1948: HMS *Nelson*, HMS *Revenge* and HMS *Rodney*. The 33,900-ton *Nelson* had been launched in June 1937, two months before her sister ship HMS *Rodney*, alongside whom she now lay for the last time. *Nelson* and *Rodney* were the only ships of the British fleet to carry sixteen-inch guns, which, apart from an experimental eighteen-inch gun tried out later aboard HMS *Furious*, were the largest guns used on any British naval vessels. Together the armaments aboard HMS *Nelson* and HMS *Rodney* were valued at £6,000,000, and for either ship to fire a triple salvo was reckoned to cost £700.

At Rosyth, which had at this time a work force of 7,000, 'Navy Days' were resumed that summer for the first time since the 1930s, and large crowds of visitors took this opportunity to see round the dockyard. There was even greater excitement in 1949 when the ships of the Home Fleet berthed at Rosyth prior to taking part in a large exercise in the North Sea. Later, in October, there was drama out in the Forth when HMS *Albion* was in collision with a Welsh collier. Both vessels were badly damaged and it took six tugs to bring the *Albion* safely upriver and manoeuvre her into Rosyth.

Work at the naval dockyard decreased during the 1950s and the workforce was reduced accordingly, but the 1960s saw a revival in Rosyth's fortunes when it was selected to refit Britain's fleet of nuclear submarines. Port Edgar on the opposite shore was less fortunate, and in 1975 it was finally closed as a naval base. In 1976 it was purchased by Lothian Regional Council and converted into a yacht marina and water-sports training centre. It is now the largest facility of its kind on the Forth, and those who use it are still reminded of its distinguished naval career during two world wars by a large commemorative granite stone. Remembrance wreaths of scarlet poppies are faithfully laid there on Armistice Sunday every November.

In 1982 Rosyth took on a sudden importance again when it was called on to outfit several small vessels for the Falklands Campaign. At the same time, the nearby munitions facility upriver on the Fife shore at Crombie Point also set a record for the quick turnaround of a naval supply vessel, as its employees worked round the clock to help defeat the Argentinean invaders.

After years of decline, the Royal Naval Dockyard at Rosyth was officially closed on 7 November 1995 when, on an appropriately dreich day, the last remaining ships of the Grey Funnel Line cast off their mooring ropes for the final time. With the rain weeping in sympathy, they sailed under the Forth Bridge and down the firth on their way to their new bases at Portsmouth and Devonport in the south of England and at Coulport on Loch Long in the Clyde Estuary.

Since then, Rosyth has been operated as a commercial dockyard by

Fig. 148

The end of the war meant the end of the sea-going careers of many British naval vessels. The battleship HMS Rodney continued in service until 1948, when she made her last voyage to the Firth of Forth to be broken up in the shadow of the Forth Railway Bridge at Inverkeithing. Together with her sister ship HMS Nelson, also scrapped at Inverkeithing the same year, the Rodney carried the largest guns mounted on any British naval vessel of the day. This picture shows her nine sixteen-inch guns, mounted in three turrets, all of which could be fired to either port or starboard. Shells for a broadside from these mighty weapons weighed almost ten tons and could hit targets out of sight over the horizon up to over forty miles distant, with spotter-planes being used to ensure that they landed on target. King George VI had previously visited HMS Rodney at Rosyth on 25 September 1945.

Basin for Submarines.
View looking *east* ~~seawards~~.
Shewing foundation walls fu
rendered necessary owing to

Intermediate Jetty.
Opening of Basin.
K
10

Babcock Engineering Ltd. As promised, the government provided it with a major naval contract: the five-year refit of the aircraft carrier HMS *Ark Royal*. This work was completed in July 2001. There was drama on the river when the huge vessel's rudder failed as she began her sea-trials, but the Admiralty was at pains to deny press reports that either the Forth Road Bridge or the cantilever railway bridge were ever in any danger of being involved in a collision. Much more seriously, however, the completion of the *Ark Royal* contract and the loss of nuclear submarine work resulted in the laying-off of 400 men, almost half of the dockyard's workforce. Rosyth being the major employer in Fife, this was a major blow to the local economy. To end on a more optimistic note, however, the following month, in August 2001, Babcock succeeded in winning a contract from the Admiralty to build forty small landing craft. The Forth's long links with the Royal Navy thus continue, at least in small measure, into the new millennium

Fig. 152
This view of Royal Navy vessels in the Firth of Forth was taken at sunset from the carriage of a train steaming across the Forth Bridge.